GRAHAM SWANN

PRISON WITHOUT BARS

A JOURNEY FROM BROKENNESS TO WHOLENESS;
FROM HOPELESSNESS TO HOPE

RIVER
PUBLISHING

River Publishing & Media Ltd
Barham Court
Teston
Maidstone
Kent
ME18 5BZ
United Kingdom

info@river-publishing.co.uk

ISBN 978-1-908393-37-1
Printed and bound by CPI Group (UK) Ltd, Croydon, CR0 4YY
Cover design by www.SpiffingCovers.com

CONTENTS

WHAT OTHERS ARE SAYING ABOUT THIS BOOK...

"The UK's relentless decline into family breakdown, random violence, 'sink' estates, drunken riots, and pointless killings has left most authorities at a loss to remedy such problems. This moving book, with its heart-stopping account of one man's history of early victimisation and vile subjection to unspeakable cruelty and abuse, is shocking.

His fears later triggered ferocity, with escalating violent responses, then clashes with the Law. Dire consequences followed. The only explanation for Graham's radical change and the freedom that restored, then tamed, this violent thug, was Christ and God's gospel that can renew everything. A truly amazing story, offering help and hope for anyone!"
Greg Haslam, Senior Minister, Westminster Chapel, London.

"Swanny's story is a great read, especially for anyone who, like Jesus, doesn't want to compartmentalise their Christianity into a conservative, middle class context. Avoiding the traps of maudlin self-pity and graphic, gratuitous scenes of sex and violence that can so easily weigh down stories of this genre, Swanny paints a clear and well-written picture of a life filled with fear, despair and hopelessness; the perfect scenario for Jesus' love to operate into.

Whether we have experienced the same depths of brokenness as he has, most people can relate to Swanny's desperate search for meaning and freedom from his past. This is a story of hope in the first degree. Jesus said 'Those who are forgiven much, love much,' and this is clearly the case with Swanny's testimony of the life-changing power of Jesus Christ to not only forgive sin, but also give a brand new life.

I loved this vivid yet economical description of a life transformed. It's a book that belongs on the shelves of anyone who is serious about bringing the truth of Jesus Christ to their sphere of influence. In fact, anyone who works in a Street Pastor type ministry would find it worth their while to buy ten copies at a time – there are a lot of people out there who could take another step of freedom into Christ by reading this powerful story."

Bev Murrill, Founder, Christian Growth International

"It has been a pleasure for me to get to know Swanny and appreciate the way he expresses his love for God. The words, 'he who has been forgiven much, loves much' come to mind. He has been an immense encouragement to the faith of many people. His spiritual insight and ability to explain deep truths with simplicity have led many people to Christ and caused many to change the pains of their past into hope for their future. This book shows that God does extraordinary things in and through ordinary people. This book is potentially life changing, but relevant and practical no matter where we are in life."

Paul Garner, Pastor of the Beacon Christian Centre

"I've known Swanny for a few years now and in that time his spiritual growth and biblical knowledge have been supernaturally quickened – as if God has his life on a fast track to greatness. I consider it an honour to be able to pass comment on the pages

of his book. Swanny writes as he thinks, with raw honesty and emotion. I love that while the opening chapters highlight his haunted past and where he has come from, the remainder of the book shows exactly what happens when the God of the universe reaches down from on high and rescues us from the gutter of our former lives. Not only is this a testimony, it is a teaching resource for anyone who has been snatched from the gates of hell and set free into the light, but who still needs guidance as to how to really live the John 10:10 life that Jesus came to give us. I highly recommend it to anyone who feels that they are imprisoned by their past."
Kate Kent, Senior Leader, The Rock Church, Nottingham

"The Swanny you meet for a curry with the blokes is a far cry from the Swanny you first meet in this book. This is the story of a radical and enduring transformation. Gritty, no-nonsense and full-on, it needs to be read by as many people as possible. Buy a copy for yourself and another for a mate. The message in this book will profoundly affect your life."
Carl Beech, International Director, CVM

ACKNOWLEDGEMENTS

I'd like to express my sincere thanks to so many of the people I've been blessed to meet on my journey. Those who have shown me kindness and love are too numerous to mention – you know who you are and I thank each and every one of you. But a few people warrant a special mention:

My beautiful wife, Rachel: thank you for always being there for me. Thank you for loving me and showering me with kindness. Words can't express what you mean to me. I love you, Rachel. Also to my beautiful kids: thank you for just being yourselves. I love you all so much.

I'd like to thank Tyler and Louise for stepping out in faith and telling me about Jesus. Thanks to Kate Kent for being such an inspiration to me. Thanks too to my close friends, Bob and Wendy, for being there for me through both my tough times and my good times.

Thanks to my long-time friend Sam Skillen for pushing me forward and for sitting for hours on end, listening as I re-wrote this book. Cheers Sam. Thanks also go to Sylvia Saunders for your precious help on the first draft. Also, thank you to my dearest and gentle friend whom I love and admire so much, Colin Stainton. Colin, if it wasn't for you mate this book would never have been published. Thank you for your gift and all your hard work.

Thank you to David Shearman for your love, friendship and kindness. Thanks also to Tim Pettingale for your gift and time spent on the book. As always, your gentle spirit goes before you – thanks mate.

I'd like to thank my Pastor, Paul Garner, for being my safety net. You've kept me focused; you're an inspiration and one of the best. You've taught me all about character building; thank you so much.

Last, but certainly not least, thanks to my Father God. Thank you for setting me free and for giving me a new spirit and hope for the future. I pray that you will use my story to change the lives of many others.

Graham Swann

FOREWORD

I have known Swanny for some years now and of all the many people I have met around the world he is one on his own – unique, dynamic and fascinating, with a compelling story, special gifts from God and a heart full of kindness and compassion.

Some of the themes of this book cover important and challenging issues that lie at the heart of human identity and personal security. Through his brokenness and sometimes harrowing, painful experiences, Swanny emerges into the uplands of human wholeness and a fulfilled life that expresses the love of Jesus.

The book is not a mild pastiche of cuddly platitudes; it sits where Swanny sits: it is real, gutsy, hard hitting, yet loving, tender and warm. You may laugh; you could very well cry; you may well believe that God has the power and ability to deal with the issues you or your wider community face. He has so amazingly helped Swanny emerge from a place of despair to be a purveyor of hope, so why could this not happen for you and yours?

If you feel deep, raw emotion at any point you will probably help yourself by stopping, reflecting and facing up to any issues that are raised in you. If you do, "the end of the matter will be better than the beginning."

Ben Okri is quoted in the book Monoculture saying,

"It is easy to forget how mysterious and mighty stories are. They do their work in silence, invisibly. They work with all the internal materials of the mind and self. They become part of you while changing you. Beware the stories you read or tell; subtly, at night, beneath the waters of consciousness they are altering your world."

This story, I believe, is one such story. It touches a wider canvas of need, often undetected or ignored, especially among the men and boys who live in Swanny's original world. Leaders of civil society, especially the faith communities, should pay more attention to its issues. The political elite, with their 3-to-5 year manifestos and plans need to find a longer term strategy. They have money, but the shaping of culture needs more than and better use of that money.

A book such as this takes us on a journey with its pain and joy, its darkness and light, its anger and peace and from brokenness to wholeness.

It is a true story but also a parable, a narrative, a signpost. It points to the most amazing rescue story ever written. God in His love comes into our damaged world, with its lost potential and sin strewn humanity, sinking in self-effort with hurt people hurting many other people.

God's love in Jesus Christ offers each of us a way out of

whatever makes us less than we were born to be. Some call it the greatest story ever told.

The place called Hope Street that Swanny found has space on it for everyone. Go and find your place!

David Shearman

PROLOGUE

We were sitting in a park on a swelteringly hot summer's day. Behind us, canal boats chugged along the willow-lined river and ducks darted in and out of their path. It was just Rachel, me and a specially prepared picnic. A cool box contained our lunch and the chilled bottle of wine was already open. Viewed from the outside it seemed like an idyllic setting: quality time with the woman I loved; a picturesque setting; a great lunch and a lazy afternoon ahead. But this superficial veneer masked a world of inner torture and turmoil.

To date my life had not so much been a journey, but rather a series of collisions and crashes. Occasional highs were wiped out by crushing lows. Childhood trauma had set the stage for a dysfunctional adult life that could never be put right without divine intervention. I had thrown myself into jobs, drink and even crime to try to forget the pain and hurt of the past, but I couldn't forget. Nothing helped. Drinking binges did nothing to remove the emotional pain – they just numbed it for a short

time. No matter what I did, I couldn't shake off my past. It was always pursuing me, creeping in the background waiting to burst out and collide with my present. Most often it came visiting at night, when the darkness and stillness suffocated me; it played endless games with my mind.

Here we were, Rachel and I, together and yet apart. It seemed to me that whenever something good, something beautiful came into my life, I would unconsciously do everything I could to sabotage it. Why would anyone do that? It was as though my life was running to a pre-programmed script that said: nothing good will ever happen to you, so don't expect it. You have no hope. If anything good does come along, it won't last. So, like some horrible, self-fulfilling prophet, I systematically hurt, pushed away and destroyed all that was good in my life. I was like a time bomb, set to self-destruct.

The child I had been haunted the man I had become. It's hard for me to explain to you how real this experience was for me. It was so much more than simply my emotions playing up or the symptoms of post traumatic stress. It was like being followed by a stalker who refused to leave me alone and who couldn't be kept at bay by a restraining order. This lost boy followed me doggedly, constantly speaking the same words to me, over and over again: "Don't tell – it's our secret. Don't be weak, Swanny."

I was with Rachel, holding her hand, fingers entwined, two hands becoming one. "I love you, Mrs Swann," I said turning to her. She looked deep into my eyes. "I love you too, Mr Swann," she said, squeezing my hand a little tighter, confirming our union. But as we spoke of our love I could already feel the child's hand on my shoulder. Tears welled in my eyes and I struggled to contain them. I desperately wanted to tell her about my past.

My heart reasoned that she wouldn't reject me, no matter what I told her or how difficult it was to stomach. But my mind raced. Reason was deafened by the lost boy's voice: "Don't tell her! You can't tell her. She will reject you and then you'll have nothing. Keep the secret – it's our secret."

"Why won't you leave me alone!" my head screamed. I wanted to talk, tell Rachel the truth, to just let it all come spilling out, but the words died in my throat. "Keep the secret, Swanny. Don't tell…" As quickly and easily as the intimacy between us blossomed, I felt myself pushing Rachel away. I was about to ruin a perfect afternoon … again. Why was I doing it, again? But the lost boy's voice persisted until I just gave in. "Don't tell … don't tell … don't tell…" If only I could find the strength to allow myself to be weak. But how?

PART ONE:
A STORY IS WRITTEN

1

A SHADOW IS CAST

The UK was enjoying an Indian Summer in the September of 1965 and my mam tells me that the sun shining through her bedroom window was warm on her face as I was born. The sunlight made my eyes squint, she says, as I blinked my way into the world. She had looked forward eagerly to this moment and now it had come – I'd arrived. We lived in a 1940s council house in Loughborough, Leicestershire – my mam, dad, and my three-year old brother. Little Tony looked on amazed as all 6lbs 10oz of me snuggled safe in the sanctuary of a pair of loving arms.

Kids grow fast and a year or so later I was taking the steps that allowed me to follow my mam wherever she went. I was an inquisitive snooper, rummaging about for love and attention; happy and contented to help her with whatever she happened to be doing. I'm sure she would have loved five minutes peace, but she took me with her everywhere she went. Nothing was too much trouble and she allowed me to trail after her all day long, giving me a welcoming smile and love in abundance.

Nevertheless, mam had a fiery temper when roused and on occasion I saw it erupt. People knew exactly where they stood with her because she told it how it was. Thankfully, as quickly as her anger boiled over, it subsided, and her rich, generous spirit would return. I cherished her.

Growing up was all about family and I still have some fine memories of those days. I was loved by so many people. There was mam, then there was Dad. Dad, who was known for his trademark dark hair, slicked back with Brylcream, and his passion for rock 'n' roll, idolised me. As someone has said, every small boy views his father as a hero, with jumbled feelings of both fear and awe. I was no different. But time with dad was scarce.

He was the wage earner in the family and he worked hard to see the colour of his money at the end of the week. After five days of hard graft he enjoyed a few pints in our local, the Bull's Head, along with the other working men, and felt he deserved it. It was a proper "spit and sawdust" drinking retreat, crammed with animated characters and jokers; industrious blokes who'd sweated through yet another shift and looked forward to some high-spirited banter. There wasn't much money around in the Midlands in the mid-sixties – at least not where we lived – but people still enjoyed life. Though Monday morning clock-in time came around all too quickly, people lived it up at the weekend, with a few beers and some laughter before stumbling home for their tea.

Many of my good memories revolve around my grandma, dad's mum. I spent many a sunny hour being fussed over at grandma Swann's house. I have fond memories of sitting with her, eating pickled onions, chatting to her about anything and nothing. During the cold months we would sit by her blistering coal fire. The distinct smell of that smoky warmth is as strong in my memory as the picture of it. She made me feel so loved. I never knew my granddad who died before I was born and to this day I know little about him. He suffered a great deal of ill health and died before his time aged just 49. Grandma Swann, however, was a fine-looking, kind-hearted lady who spoke with a Suffolk accent. She had moved from Lowestoft to Loughborough during the war and raised nine children there, including my dad.

Time with my other set of grandparents was often spent during trips to east coast seaside towns like Skegness and Mablethorpe. In those days it felt like the school holidays lasted for an eternity. The memories of those days also bring back all the departed senses that accompanied them. The scent of sizzling bacon drifting over the caravan park and my grandma calling me for breakfast; the smell of toast made with real butter. As far as I knew, my grandma made the best toast in the world. I once said to mam, "It doesn't taste the same at our house. Why?" She gave me an odd look and replied cryptically, "I didn't think it would!"

Sometimes, when I'm sitting alone with just a mug of tea for company, I think back to these flawless days – a kid with no cares, setting off on a bright new day; the optimistic excitement I had about the adventures that lay ahead with my bucket and spade. I try to recapture those feelings of innocence. I was a small boy with nothing to worry about and everything to look forward to.

My maternal grandma reminded me of Hilda Ogden from Coronation Street. She had a tiny Yorkshire Terrier who she appeared to love more than my granddad. "She thinks it's human," mam would whisper to me. The little dog was very protective of grandma and would snarl whenever anyone approached her.

Granddad was a pint-sized man who was never without a pipe and the smell of his Condor tobacco still lingers. He was extremely fond of a drop of rum too. He used to tell me stories about his time in the war, such as the occasion when he and some mates had been given water to drink that was contaminated to the point of being poisonous. Out of his group of ten, all nine of his mates died; only he survived. Allegedly, the doctors told him that because his stomach was coated with rum it had diluted the effects of the poison. I don't know whether there is any truth in that tale, but as a small boy I listened in awe. He was an old school sailor, covered in tattoos and full of similar ripping yarns. He never tired of chatting to me and I looked at him with love and admiration. "When I grow up, I'm going to be like granddad and have lots of tattoos," I told mam. She just laughed.

* * *

A shadow was cast over these sunny, happy days when I was about 10 years old. Things changed for everybody, including me, and not for the better. The innocence and simplicity of our former existence became troubled and pressured. I began to lose my naivety and see that life wasn't as carefree as I'd imagined. My brother, Tony, began to bring distress and anxiety into the family. He was always fighting and beginning to get into trouble for breaking into properties. I remember he would often run away from home too. I didn't understand why. One minute I was a happy kid, content with life, then almost overnight life became tainted. Circumstances out of my control began to intrude.

The effect all this had on mam and dad was both immense and

very obvious to me. I was frightened by it, increasingly anxious, but I didn't say how I felt. They say you can't put an old head on young shoulders and it's true. The little boy who'd known such joyful times was now witnessing those he loved being battered by life's storms and life at home worsened steadily. Dad didn't cope well with situations like this and the slump in his shoulders each day told the story. "He suffers with his nerves," I was told, and "it runs in the Swann family." My folks tried to make light of it: "All us Swanns suffer with it," they would chuckle, but it was no laughing matter. Behind the jovial words was a darker reality – one which I would have first hand experience of in the not-too-distant future.

I remember the day when things came to a head. Appropriately, it was raining. A torrential downpour assaulted the streets of Loughborough. Men were running holding newspapers over their heads and women huddled under umbrellas. I ran home from school as fast as my legs would carry me. Entering the house, I sensed the heavy atmosphere. Mam was crying, her head in her hands. I went to see what was the matter.

"Your dad's had a breakdown," she sobbed, her tears flowing freely, the corners of her mouth quivering with emotion.

I looked at her blankly. I had no idea what a "breakdown" was. I followed her gaze out of the window and caught sight of my dad at the bottom of the garden. He was wandering around like a lost soul, shaven-headed, staring at the ground. All his beautiful black hair was gone. He'd shaved it all off while I was at school. His shoulders looked more bowed than normal, as though they were carrying the weight of mankind on them. I could see his mouth forming words.

"Who's he talking to mam?" I asked. Punctuated by sobs, her

broken reply came back: "He's talking to his dad…"

"Talking to his dad?" I repeated. "But…" I broke off, leaving the obvious unsaid: his dad's dead. Mam nodded.

So here I was: Tony was mostly absent, mam was heartbroken, sobbing uncontrollably. Now my dad, the man I treasured with all my heart, was standing in the pouring rain talking to someone who'd been dead for twelve years. My world was plunged into confusion.

Life was never the same again. Dad never really recovered and Tony continually brought aggravation home. The police were regular visitors, knocking on our door at all hours. Mam and dad tried to insulate me from the stress as best they knew how, bundling me into the back room so I didn't have to listen to the difficult conversations. But all it did was fuel my insecurities. They were trying to protect their youngest son, I know, but it felt as though everyone had stopped loving me. This wasn't true, of course, but I felt unloved, alone and frightened. The quiet calm and confidence I had known until then were gradually being replaced with uncertainty, self-doubt and a lack of confidence. Gone was the innocence; gone was the happy naivety.

Alongside the dawning reality that my formerly safe, secure, family environment was crumbling, I was being bullied. It had started a couple of months earlier. Maybe I would have spoken up about it in different circumstances. But because of the turmoil at home, where everyone was consumed with their own problems, I stayed silent. The feelings of insecurity I felt were surfacing at school and the other kids had begun to pick up on it. I became vulnerable, a target for those who were inclined to be hurtful and unkind. Cracks appeared and my smiles turned to tears. Soon I became the headline attraction for the warped amusement of others.

It began with childish name calling, but the nastier kids soon elevated that to intimidation. From there it became a game: terrorise the easy target; get the scrawny lad who you could give a good kicking. At first it was shoving, needless confrontation, the odd punch in the face; eventually it was just sheer evil. I was beaten on a daily basis and forced to hand over my pocket money.

I was small for my age and skinny. Frail in body, but now in mind too. The bullies robbed me of the last vestiges of my self-confidence. Now each day was to be approached with fear and dreaded anticipation, instead of my former carefree optimism. I was immersed in a world where others controlled my thoughts, manipulated my actions, and had a hold over my life.

Too many abusive occasions to recall here resulted in perverted entertainment for others and depression for me. Regularly I was marched to an area of Loughborough called Beacon Hill – around 300 acres of parkland mainly consisting of grass and woodland. Beacon Hill is an area of great natural beauty and a place rich in history. For me, however, it was the crucible of my pain and suffering, where I was humiliated and tortured.

Tortured is a strong word, I realise, but I can only describe it as that. The bullies abused not just my body, but my mind. Frequently I was ordered to strip down to my pants and run. I was given a head start and then hunted down like a terrified fox. They pursued me, chanting and shouting. I never managed to outrun them, not once. When caught I was thrashed with branches; hounded like prey and then whipped. To them I was a parasite, a cockroach that needed stamping on.

If it wasn't Beacon Hill then it was New Walks, another area close to where I lived. It was a shadowy, damp place, thick with oak trees, with a small brook running alongside. There used to be a rope swing tied to one of the branches of a huge oak tree. It was here that I was brutalised. There were a group of boys who seemed to share a passion for the mistreatment of others and spent as much time as they could inflicting misery on the helpless. They would tie my hands tightly with the rope and then push me down the hill. My cries went unheeded as I tumbled down, unable to break my fall, the rope cutting into my wrists. Then, even as I pleaded for mercy, they would beat me with sticks. My back and ribs throbbed and all I could think was, "Please, let me die."

* * *

It's strange how our minds work. As adults, unresolved issues from our past, wanted or unwanted, refuse to lie down and die. Here I was, a grown man, waking up to another day that would be dominated by the lost boy of my past. The unspoken trauma that I had obediently kept a secret drained the life out of my existence. This ominous silence hung over me, subdued me, suffocated me. Those painful days had come and gone, but emotionally I was still in the thick of them.

This day I'd got up and padded into the bathroom for a shower after a heavy night – just one more in a string of heavy nights. Studying my reflection in the mirror all I could think was, "You're pathetic." The previous night the TV had droned on till the early hours, entertaining a large collection of empty beer cans while I lay unconscious. I was severely depressed about the way my life had turned out. Beer, all too fleetingly, took that feeling away. In truth, I had such deep feelings of utter vulnerability that no amount of beer ever helped. No one understood. Rachel couldn't understand why I insisted on drinking so much. Why would she? She didn't know because I hadn't told her. I was trapped in a cycle of pain followed by numbness, followed by more pain.

I took my shower. It felt like just a few minutes elapsed as my mind turned things over. In reality 40 minutes passed by. Have a Nice Day by the Stereophonics was playing on the radio when I walked into the kitchen. It reminded me of the time I'd first met Rachel – that smile, the slight tilt of her head, and those eyes. I made myself a cup of tea. We had six chairs in the kitchen-diner but I only ever used one. I slumped down in my usual spot. "Snap out of it, Swanny." I'd heard those words a thousand times. It was some people's pat answer to what they perceived as my "problem". But my depression was getting worse. There was no way I was going to simply snap out of it.

My mind travelled the same tired, worn out territory as before. There had been the bullies and then there had been him – the man who had further sought to rob me of my innocence and extinguish any last spark of hope. "I should have done something," I chided myself for the thousandth time. I'd been saying this for years, repeatedly, day-in-day-out.

Naturally, I couldn't forgive them – I hated them all, the bullies and him. Hate barely described the revulsion I felt for them. But then I couldn't forgive myself either. I was angry at them for taking my life away and leaving me with derelict emotions, but I was equally angry at myself for allowing it.

Living daily with the fallout had exhausted me and was exhausting those around me who had to witness it. I drove people away from me. I couldn't bring myself to trust anyone – even the most loving, caring people around me who showed me nothing but kindness. I was beyond help.

I finished the dregs of my tea and looked out of the kitchen window. "How ironic," I thought. No matter how depressed and confused I felt inside, the garden was always the complete opposite: neat, well ordered, with not a blade of grass out of place. "If only my life looked like that." I caught sight of my reflection in the glass. I looked dead behind the eyes, I thought. Eleven forty-five came around quickly and I had done nothing with my day but relive my past. Maybe it was time to lay at least one of my ghosts to rest, I thought.

That man – one of the most "influential" people in my life, in the worst possible way – who still exerted so much control over my daily life, even though he was long gone. A part of me had died because of him. I needed to either reclaim that part or completely let go of it if I was ever to move forward with life. Yes, I had been terrorised and bullied, but I had never told a soul that I had also been sexually abused. I knew that someday, somehow, I had to confront my terror and acknowledge what had happened. I couldn't carry on living like this, with a volcano of rage simmering just below the surface. I'd boiled over many times, but I was getting much worse.

Something had to give.

2

DARKNESS FALLS

It's funny what we believe as kids. As far as we are concerned, whatever our parents say is gospel and we often carry those beliefs into adulthood – whether or not there is any substance in them. "If you spill the salt, throw it over your shoulder into the eyes of the devil," my mam used to tell me. My childhood was jam-packed with such superstitious sayings or habits designed to ward off bad luck. My mam probably learnt them from her mam and then unwittingly passed them on to me. These false notions, however, became ingrained in me and followed me into adulthood, whether I liked it or not.

As a kid, whenever I was going somewhere I would sprint from one lamppost to the next as quickly as I could. I told myself, "If I get to this one faster, all my problems will get better." I obsessively crossed my fingers each day, believing, hoping that all my bad luck would go away. Later, as an adult, if I suspected misfortune was coming my way I would instinctively cross my fingers behind my back, as if this action had the power to avert disaster. Guess what – it never did. No amount of finger-crossing or salt in the eyes of the devil prevented the bullies from victimising me. Day in and day out they beat me; thrashed and hammered me until my body throbbed and my bones ached and cried out for respite.

Each night I lay in the darkness of my bedroom reflecting on the day's events. The darkness threatened to engulf me, swallow me whole. My body ached alright, but that was nothing compared to the ache that had formed inside. I was drowning in sorrow. With each day that passed I died a little more inside. Each night I prayed for some kind of deliverance from the hands of my torturers.

One particular day began like so many others. The gang of bullies was on my tail once again and I had been pursued like a dog across some fields. But after the expected beating and kicking they had devised a new form of sick punishment. They dragged me to a spot in the field they'd discovered where there was something resembling a crater in the ground. It was a large hole, filled with manure.

It was the height of summer and the sun's rays had baked a hardened crust over the top of this pit. Underneath it would be like coagulated syrup. The lads thought it would provide some great entertainment for them if I was forced to walk across the crust, to see if it would bear my weight. Fear began to rise up in me and panic coursed through my body. I was shoved forward by one of the ring leaders. It was like being forced to walk the plank. I either had to walk into an uncertain fate or I would be beaten mercilessly. I stumbled forward.

I'd only taken a few steps when my shoes began to stick and the crust groaned and shifted. I pleaded with my tormentors to let me turn back, but they laughed and ordered me to go on. The surface began to subside and every step I took made matters worse. My progress became laboured and I began to be sucked down, my legs fighting helplessly against the viscous treacle. I was sinking fast. Every movement I made worsened my situation and the more I struggled the more I was eaten up by the pit. My heart was pounding so hard I could feel it in my head. The more I tried to free myself, the deeper I went until eventually I fell forward.

The gang were revelling in this top entertainment, literally rolling with laughter – that is until I started screaming. I had reached the point where the possibility of being completely sucked under was very real. I was being overwhelmed and I feared for my life. I was minutes away from inevitable suffocation. Time stood still as the realisation hit home. The yelling and laughter was abruptly terminated and I could see expressions of terror on the gangs' faces, mirroring my own. They understood that things had gone too far – horribly wrong, in fact. "Help!" I screamed. But no one helped. No one wanted to be implicated in the tragedy of another boy's death. Like the pathetic, weak bullies they were, every last one turned and ran, leaving me to my fate.

I gave out one last desperate scream for help and was amazed to find a strong hand grabbing the scruff of my neck. The farmer whose field it was had happened to be nearby and came to investigate the noise. He saved my life – but he didn't do so cheerfully. He bawled me out and gave me a good telling off for being so stupid. "You're lucky I was passing!" he fumed. "You could have been killed." I didn't have the energy to tell him it wasn't my fault I was there. After dragging me out of the pit he ordered me to get off his land and added that he'd take a pot shot at me with his gun if I ever trespassed again.

I began to really hate my life. I felt alone, afraid, isolated and abandoned. The repeated application of trauma had scarred my mind and bruised my soul. I genuinely believed that no one loved me – not even my family. When bad things consistently happen to us we tell ourselves, even subconsciously, that there must be something defective in us for others to want to treat us this way. How easily we take on the sins of others and internalise them, feeling that we are the ones to blame, that somehow we are bringing this on ourselves.

So my existence was marked by feelings of abandonment, pain and now there was shame and guilt too. I felt as though I was merely surviving life; unaccompanied, unsupported and unloved.

* * *

At home, my brother Tony was getting into so much trouble that he was on the brink of being taken into care. The turmoil this caused in the family home meant that my problems had largely slipped by unnoticed. That began to change when I started losing weight. I hardly ate anything because I never felt hungry. Stress and worry had killed my appetite and it was beginning to show. I was a small kid with a small frame to start with, but now I was skin and bone and Mam noticed and took me to see the doctor.

I also began to follow in Tony's footsteps and started getting into problems at school as my troubled existence began to spill over into other areas of my life. Mam was constantly being called in to see one of my teachers or the headmaster. I think the teachers got bored with trying to whack some sense into me with a plimsoll. To me it was nothing compared with the beatings I was receiving outside of school.

My P.E. teacher told me that I was a good swimmer with lots of potential, stronger than most, but I hated it. By then I didn't want to draw any attention to myself if at all possible. Standing out was a sure fire way to get knocked down, I had learnt. My school at Shelthorpe was one of the few that had its own swimming pool at the time, but I wasn't interested. Of course, the fact that I was gifted at something and yet refused to pursue it agitated my teachers all the more. Eventually their patience with me wore thin and, like so many kids before me, I was "written off", told in no uncertain terms that I would never achieve anything with my life. "Fools like you never do," one teacher eloquently put it. So that was it – another lie embedded in my soul. Another line of code added to the program that would ensure my life pursued a downward spiral.

* * *

The school bell rang loudly, cutting across the general hubbub of the classroom. For most kids it signified the end of another day. For me it was like the "final lap" bell at the Olympics – the signal to sprint – or maybe the starting bell in a boxing match: seconds away, round two...

I gazed at the clock on the classroom wall and counted the minutes, the seconds, anticipating the sound of the bell. When it rang I hit the ground running, my only thought to sprint out of the playground as fast as I could. If there was even the slightest chance of me gaining a head start on my pursuers I was going to grab it and run for the safety of home.

Today I began my usual dash, across the playground and out of the gates as fast as my skinny legs would carry me. All the time I was looking over my shoulder, afraid that the bullies were onto me. I ran as fast and as hard as I could, fuelled by adrenalin, until I was sure – completely sure – that I had put enough distance between me and them to make good my escape. Gradually I slowed down, heart thudding, wiping the sweat from my face, relieved that today was one of the days when I'd evaded capture.

I was nearly home, still shooting the occasional glance over my shoulder, when I heard a gruff voice calling to me. "Oi! What are you looking at?" I stopped in my tracks, panic rising, thinking that maybe a bully had taken a different route to cut me off – but it didn't sound like a boy's voice. I looked around and there he was, an ugly giant of a man with bulging eyes standing in the doorway to his house. For some reason his stare arrested my progress and I felt glued to the spot. After what seemed like a long time I spoke in a trembling voice: "Nothing."

"Come here," he ordered. His face was expressionless.

I didn't speak, but I shook my head.

"Come here," he said again, voice softening slightly. I shook my head again, but he persisted.

"Come here, I want to show you something."

I don't know why, but I felt as though he had some power over me. I didn't want to see whatever it was he wanted to show me; I didn't want to go into his house. Yet I made my way tentatively down his path. He towered over me, a monstrous figure, eclipsing me. "Come on lad, hurry up," he said and seconds later I was stepping inside his house for the first time.

* * *

The following morning was dreary. Outside it was drizzling with rain. It was cold in my room and the condensation gathered on the inside of my window. "Graham, get up or you'll be late for school," I heard mam shouting from downstairs. I muffled her hollering by pulling the blankets over my head.

The previous night I had cried myself to sleep. I'd spent sleepless hours praying for relief; praying to a God that I didn't know whether or not I believed in. Last night I'd begged Him to let me die, but He hadn't granted my request. Yesterday I had avoided the bullies and escaped a beating, but I had been plunged into a new world of confusion and suffering. The big man with the bulging eyes had used me and I had the inescapable, sinking feeling that today was going to be the same as yesterday. I had begged him to stop, but he'd ignored me. I was just a scared, 10-year old bullied kid with no confidence and no self-worth. He was strong and determined to have his depraved appetite fulfilled. Something told me that I would be seeing him again very soon. I felt powerless to stop it.

3

THE TIDE TURNS

I had become the prey of a predatory paedophile; a victim of sexual abuse. There are no words to describe how I felt as I walked away from my abuser's house. One minute I was sprinting home, pleased to have evaded capture for once, the next I was caught in a new trap. My life changed forever that day.

My captor instructed me to go upstairs and ordered me to lie on his bed and close my eyes. I was so terrified that fear immobilised me. I couldn't move. I was aware of the stale, musty stench of his bedroom; I listened to the creak of the floorboards as he went to the bedroom door and clicked it shut. He put a pillow over my head and I just lay there like a corpse until he had finished using me. I wanted my mam to come and save me, but I knew I was alone, helpless to stop it.

My abuser had something in common with my bullies. He'd chanced his arm to try and exploit me and had immediately seen my weakness and vulnerability. He must have been delighted that I didn't have the self-confidence to resist him. On the inside

I was a mess – confused, full of anxiety, weak and isolated – and it showed on the outside. Every beating I received and every touch from the hands of this pervert drove me deeper within myself until I became the lost boy who was destined to haunt the grown man.

Both my bullies and this evil man seized upon my fear. They held such power over me. I hated myself for letting them get away with it. The bullies controlled me by force and intimidation. It had been proven beyond doubt that I wasn't strong enough to resist them – not now, not ever – so the pattern had been set and they would ensure it continued. My abuser controlled me by destroying every last shred of self-worth. He played his power game with me every day. He told me that I was ugly and that nobody loved me. He said he would kill me if I didn't do what he wanted or if I dared to tell anyone.

Some reading this might think, why didn't you stop it? Why didn't you avoid this man, run away, tell someone what was happening? The truth is, I felt absolutely powerless to do anything, such was my lack of self-worth and self-confidence. Maybe, had I had the support and security of a strong home behind me, things would have been different. But I was vulnerable, exposed, and so low and desperate that these people succeeded in exerting their wills upon me and I just crumbled and gave in. I was only 10-years old. I didn't know what to do.

I walked to his house every day after school. He was always waiting at his front door, looking for me. My emotions were crushed again and again by the sense of impending doom, seeing this dirty man who was about to molest me, standing there waiting eagerly for his cheap sexual satisfaction. My legs shook with fear. I was a defenceless little kid. All I wanted was a hug from my mam, but each day this commanding figure would give out his orders. I'd cross my fingers every time, hoping that today would be different, that today it might not happen. But every day for three years that pillow was placed over my head and I would smell his bad breath and body odour. Those smells lived with me for more than 30 years.

After three years of abuse I was an emotional husk. On the outside I looked like any other kid entering his teens, but on the inside there was nothing. I was dead behind the eyes. Day in and day out I was molested by a faceless beast who only cared about one thing, his perverted self-gratification. He didn't give a second thought to the consequences of his actions and what that meant for the little boy with a pillow covering his head. For all his dominance and power over me he could never look me in the eyes and risk seeing his own diseased reflection. All I could do was to try and run away in my mind, even though my body could not escape.

Three and a bit years... that man abused me over a thousand times. It's unimaginable when set down on paper – a cold, mathematical figure. To me it felt like a thousand lifetimes. Each touch on my innocent body was like the cut of a knife, further engraving the pain into my soul. Later, as reaching my teens ushered in a move to a new school and a new routine, I would eventually escape from his clutches. But after three years of abuse, he had inflicted a lifetime's emotional damage. The physical abuse may have ended, but his control over my mind and emotions would hold me captive for years to come.

During my early years at Garendon High School I was still being bullied in school and abused out of it. It seemed that my very existence consisted only of others taking advantage of me in one way or another. My teachers knew nothing of what was happening. They just witnessed the fallout and, as far as they were concerned, I was the disruptive kid who was heading for skid row. The school had a reputation for placing high expectations on its pupils and today describes itself as "vibrant and happy", a place where "students make good progress". Vibrant and happy were not words that described me. I was a shadow; an isolated, troubled kid. I decided on my first day that I hated the place — that was my mind set from day one. I felt that the teachers gave out mixed messages, on the one hand trying to encourage me to do better and behave, and on the other hand labelling me "hopeless". It did nothing to bolster my confidence or prevent me from becoming more fearful and solitary.

But there came a certain day at Garendon when everything changed and my life took a new direction. From nowhere a single incident caused a change of perspective and the tide turned. Here's how it unfolded:

One of my long-time bullies had cornered me, just me and him. I was subjected to the usual verbal abuse and then the physical abuse started on its normal, escalating scale: first the prodding in the chest, then the pushing and shoving, then a quick distraction to cause me to glance away and drop my guard so that the beating could properly begin. He pummelled my face with a volley of punches.

Quite suddenly a bigger, older lad appeared — someone I knew from down my street. He happened to come round the corner just as the bully landed another cheek-splitting punch on me. Without hesitation the older lad confronted the bully. "Oi!" he shouted, "Try throwing that same punch at me." The bully froze with fear, suddenly unsure of himself, not knowing what to do.

Time stood still, replaced by pregnant silence. "Come on!" he repeated, "Let's see you do that to me." In that instant I felt as though I had been released from my nightmare. My tormentor was frozen with fear; immobilised. I couldn't believe what I was seeing. I read the same terror in him that had been familiar to me for so long.

It was as though someone had reached inside me and flicked off the "victim" switch. I was euphoric. The adrenalin pumped and I was filled with joy. For the first time in living memory I experienced the feeling of power. And I loved it. My rescuer shoved the bully around, roughed him up a bit and threatened him. If he was ever caught near me again he'd have my mate to deal with. At that moment the bully appeared to me to be so much smaller than I'd realised before. I was used to being the victim, the bullied, the abused. In a second all that changed.

"Come on," the big lad said, "Let's get out of here." We walked off together. A torrent of different emotions were running through me. I tried to play it cool. I didn't know how much this lad had seen, whether or not he knew I'd had a pasting and been humiliated. "What was all that about, Swanny?" he enquired. "I don't know," I lied. "He often starts on me for no reason." I tried to make it sound as though it was no big deal. I don't think I was convincing anyone – him or me. "Not any more mate," he replied. "Nobody can do anything to you if you stand up for yourself. Don't let anyone say or do anything to you again – it's as simple as that."

And it was. From that day on, from somewhere, I don't know where, I found a new determination. No one was ever going to touch me again – no bully, no sexual abuser – and it felt amazing. I felt so free … at long last. This turning point brought with it a brand new confidence. From that day forward, not a single person bothered me again. But at what cost? I had been beaten down, bullied, abused and oppressed for years. But though I was no longer a victim, I'd crossed over to the dark side. I had become the aggressor. I was set to become the one thing that I had despised for so long: a bully.

The change in my character was rapid and spread like an uncontrollable rash. I became no better than my tormentors. And yet, it was addictive.

I became reckless. If anyone had the temerity to front up to me then I would let them have it. I dished out the violence and found that I was pretty good at it. I exercised my newfound power and enjoyed my new status. Now I had some control – and I fully intended to take advantage of anyone who displayed the same vulnerability I once did. It takes one to know one, right? I could smell fear a mile off. I was able to dominate those who were helpless and I'd be lying if I said I didn't enjoy it for all it was worth. After feeling so powerless, so weak, I now felt invincible – at least on the outside. Don't get me wrong, nothing much had changed inside. I was still that weak, frightened little kid, the one who had been controlled, manipulated and tossed around like a rag doll. But at least now I could hit back. Now I could protect myself and prevent it from happening any more.

My schooling was coming to an unnatural end. I'd taken an unpleasant liking to being the kid who now stood up for himself. This attitude had now seen me thrown out of secondary school mid-way through my third year. I was getting out of control and, like my brother, beginning to get into trouble with the police. I was taught how to street fight by older lads who could see that I was always up for it. The success fed my ego. What I couldn't see was that I was heading in the same direction as Tony – something I had never wanted to put my parents through. It sneaked up on me and I never saw it coming. Now dad was moaning at me too. "You're just as bad as your brother!" he'd say, and so I lived up to my name.

I was turning into someone I no longer recognised in the mirror. I didn't care about anything and I walked a precarious tightrope that stretched across life and death. It was a dangerous place to be. I learnt to swagger around, an arrogant kid, giving everyone the evil eye. I respected no one and cared little if I lived or died.

Time had flown. So far my journey had taken me from the innocent child who loved to visit his grandma and eat her hot buttered toast, to the kid who was bullied, a victim to be used and abused, to the messed up hard kid who enjoyed dishing it out to others. I had constructed a wall around myself, a barricade so high that even I had trouble looking in. I told myself over and over that no one was allowed to get into my space – no one. The bigger and uglier the wall looked the better it suited me. I actually believed that I was simply standing up for myself. In fact, my entire life was centred on my own fears and anxieties, my own failings. I had replaced one prison with another of my own making. I was handcuffed to a life I knew nothing about. Gone was the carefree kid; gone was the bullied kid. Here came the cheerless, stone-hearted, violent monster.

4

A CHANCE TO CHANGE

Looking back now, it is difficult for me to recount this next period of my life. I'm not proud of so many things I did during this time. But, I want to show you a few snapshots, if only to highlight the change that has taken place in me between then and now. I don't wish to glamourise the violence that became a part of my life, but I will mention some incidents to illustrate how amazingly the grace of God can work in a person's life.

Day by day, the simmering rage that for years had been held captive within me was coming to the surface and boiling over. Over time I moved far beyond simply sticking up for myself, getting into fights on the basis of self-defence. I relished violence. I enjoyed inflicting pain on others. I sought out people to bang heads with and I didn't need any provocation. I was like an explosion waiting to happen. I did my talking with my fists; they were my answer to everything.

I started to go boxing training with a mate of mine, Sam Skillen. He was an Irish lad, taller than me, rough and ready, and with a cheeky grin. He also had the same hard, reckless streak as me. Both of us trained hard and learned to fight well. I knew how to land a punishing blow. Young lads often take up boxing to get rid of pent up aggression. It didn't work that way for us. Once we had finished a training session, Sam and I would make our way over to the Loughborough University campus and find some students to pick a fight with. We wanted to practice what we'd learnt.

The progression from tearaway to thug was a quick one. Once we were in a town centre chip shop when Sam decided to punch an innocent man who was standing in the queue. Sam floored him, but then we carried on as if nothing had happened, collected our chips and left. We were walking up the road laughing about it when we heard someone yelling after us, "Come here!" Another bloke had seen what had happened and wanted to challenge us about it. Both of us dropped our chips and set on him. The ferocity of the attack was uncalled for – it usually was – as we punched and kicked him hard. Just then, a police car came around the corner. We were caught and arrested. It turned out that the man we'd just beaten up was a police officer. I was sentenced to community work. Sam was sent to Borstal.

I was still a teenager, but I had the mind of a fighter double my age. I was getting physically stronger all the time, but I was also fuelled by anger, resentment and bitterness. I was bitter about the hand I felt life had dealt me. I felt utter hatred and revulsion towards those who had overpowered me and, because of that, would never let any situation in life go. If I felt someone or something was challenging me in any way, I had to do something about it. Very often it was me who caused the strife in the first place. I had an overwhelming fear inside me – fear of being overpowered, abused. It filled me with anxiety because I couldn't have handled anything bad happening to me again. So I became the bad. I became the ferocious answer to the problem and attacked it with venom.

Home life was increasingly disordered. My brother, Tony, was eventually taken into care and I was increasingly distant from mam and dad as I followed a similar path. In my few short years I'd had a lot to cope with. I'd had to face bullying, physical and mental torture, sexual abuse and the erosion of family life. Each of these had caused its own mental scarring. Each was another reason to keep the real me locked up and unleash the violent me on the world in an effort to hit back.

The next few years, therefore, sailed by on a tide of violence. I was like a magnet who pulled other, like-minded, kids towards me. We were attracted to one another; we dealt with life in a similar way. Each of us was suffering the effects of some kind of dysfunctional past. Some shared bits and pieces of what had gone on; others just kept it to themselves. But we all had our reasons for behaving as we did. We all put a brave face on it, though inside we were hurting and confused. We attempted to help each other through life during those early years, but at the same time we were our own worst enemies.

I suppose we responded to life as the immature young people we were. We created a defence mechanism for avoiding hurt: causing it. Our behaviour was little better than animals. We cared about nothing – especially not the feelings of the poor people we nearly battered to death. I mean that statement literally. I had learnt how to box. Next I learnt how to street fight: how to take a punch; how to deliver a dirty punch in return;

how to intimidate others and never back down. It didn't matter how big, how tough or how old the other person was or, for that matter, what reputation they had as a hard hitter. I had an inflated sense of self-importance and bravado. I would literally take on anyone, no matter what. On one occasion I heard there was a particular lad who wanted to fight me. I acted on this information immediately. I found out where he lived and went round to his house. First I smashed every one of his windows, then I smashed down his front door with a baseball bat. Suddenly he didn't want to fight me any more. He fled out the back door while I was breaking in.

Sam and another mate, Brian Molloy – another lad from an Irish family – both had older brothers: John Skillen and Andy Molloy. John and Andy were both skilled fighters and boxing coaches. They also worked the doors at pubs and clubs around town and had fearsome reputations. These were my mentors when it came to honing our fighting skills. Sam was a skilful fighter and had managed to pick up some knowledge of mixed martial arts. By contrast, Brian, a big well-built lad, was an aggressive, reckless fighter who would terrorise others. He could finish the job just as quickly as he started it. Another companion around this time was Roy Jarvis – another big lad who'd moved to Loughborough from Yorkshire. Like me, Roy would never back down from a confrontation. On many occasions I would start a fight that I couldn't finish and Roy frequently had to jump in and help me.

Besides friends, I found something else to get me through these troubled years. Drink. I actually thought it was helping me at the time. It took years for me to figure out that alcohol wasn't relieving my problems but fuelling them. While we were underage Sam and I would find a quiet corner in a park and drink cider someone had bought for us. When we were older and frequented the pubs with the rest of our gang, we drank copious amounts of anything – from beer to spirits, and especially vodka.

I tried unsuccessfully to drink myself into another life. A bit of a drink didn't achieve much. A lot of drink succeeded in numbing the emotional pain – for a short time. I felt anaesthetised. But rather than provide a welcome distraction from the violence, ultimately it made things worse. After downing a string of pints I felt invincible, bullet proof. It furnished me with a false braveness and that led to a fearless reputation, which I never felt I deserved.

I'd been kicked out of my current secondary school by now and could easily have not bothered with an education, but I briefly attended Burleigh College where my life continued to be a prolonged disaster. I'd been given one last chance to change my ways and get some qualifications. But, I resisted. My time at Burleigh was a period of constant fighting with a bad attitude against those in authority. I persisted with being the bad kid on the block; the trouble-maker who took nothing seriously. "Why should I?" I reasoned. I had been crushed by life; mistreated and abused. "What do my teachers know?" I thought I knew better.

I decided, before attending a single day there, that I would gain nothing from Burleigh, so I didn't last long there. I didn't want to learn stuff from books when I was experiencing – had already experienced so much of – the rawness of life on the street. I'd already lived through more trauma than most of my teacher's put together had known in their lives. So I fought. I fought the system. I fought other kids. I drove my fists into the face of many a kid whose only crime was turning up for school that day. I didn't care and that was that. Eventually my schooling reached its own conclusion when I was expelled. My relationship with education was over.

There were few options open to me now. It was either be absorbed into the care system or enrol on a work experience programme. The latter was a poor excuse for work and really just another system to try to deal with unruly youths. Within a few weeks I found myself tending graves at Loughborough Cemetery. I cut the grass, looked after the flowers and back-filled people's graves after the funeral was over. Some days I felt like I was digging my own grave.

* * *

Another year filled with the same brutality passed whilst working at the cemetery. Nothing much had changed. As much as I believed I was growing up, in fact I was still a lost 10-year-old lad inside. One consequence of my lifestyle was a growing paranoia. This expressed itself in a number of ways, but the biggest of all was a lack of trust. The streets taught me to trust no one. This may well have worked on the streets, but it made it nigh impossible for me to develop any kind of normal relationship with anyone.

This became very evident the day I met Lesley. I knew her brother, Trev, from school. He was my age; Lesley was older. I was round at his house after school one day and he told me that Lesley liked me. She was a whole three years older than me and that made me feel kind of cool. She had bleached blonde hair and was working somewhere in town. We hit it off straight away and formed a relationship. Since she was working she was able to buy me drinks and she drank plenty herself. I became hooked on her ability to make me feel wanted, accepted, loved even.

She made me feel needed, important.

I felt cared for and I liked Lesley a lot, but I can't exactly say that I loved her back. I hadn't got a clue what love was all about. Lesley cared for me but I repaid her care with paranoia. I was full of mistrust for this girl. I was completely insecure. Because of this we had an on/off relationship that lurched from one crisis to the next before miraculously limping on. Sometimes I didn't want her and sometimes she didn't want me. But mostly it was me who was the stone-hearted one. I had to ensure that nothing penetrated my heart and had a chance of hurting me. So what hope did this girl have of really touching me? None. I pushed her away at every opportunity, yet when she pushed me away in return, I just turned my back. My emotional barricade was far too extreme to be penetrated.

My teens were rapidly disappearing. I was 17 now; grown up or so I thought. I was in the pubs all the time and, as a result, stepped up into a new league in terms of trouble and violence. It was a whole new ball game.

On one occasion, fuelled by drink, I caught sight of a lad on the other side of the pub. He was much older than me and as soon as I laid eyes on him I recognised him as one of my former bullies. Anger boiled up inside me and I knew I had to deal with this situation. I approached him and, without hesitation, thrust the pint glass I was holding into his face, shattering it. He staggered backwards and I leaped on him, stamping on him repeatedly until he was unconscious. Roy was with me at the time. "What was all that about, Swanny?" he asked after we'd made our way out of there. I tried to laugh the incident off: "Oh, he tripped me up one time."

"Well, I don't know what you'd have done if he'd really upset you," Roy commented, amazed.

I didn't want to tell him the real reason – I was too ashamed. At the time I felt no remorse for what I'd done. This was my world. You mixed your anger with half a dozen pints and the result was mindless violence. The only rule we lived by was that there were no rules.

On another occasion a big group of football fans came to Loughborough and found their way into one of our regular pubs. I walked in and realised there were about 30 out-of-towners. Without a thought I shoved my way right into the middle of them and threw a pint glass at one lad's head. I was laughing and shouting, "Come on, let's have it!" A split second later the punches were flying. I enjoyed the buzz of a good fight. Sam and John Skillen were already in the pub and dived in too, otherwise I might have been killed. Once again my mates had to help me out. I had a reputation for not caring if I won or lost.

We made money any way we could. This meant taking part in muggings, robbery and dealing in stolen goods down the pub, buying and selling. Sam and I were routinely armed with knives and coshes. We'd pull knives on unsuspecting lads around our age and demand money. On one occasion we had no money for a drink, so my brother Tony went into the local amusement arcade, pulled out a knife and demanded all the money from the till. Shortly after he came out I went in to further threaten the staff with a knife and tell them that if they reported us to the police I'd be back to cut their tongues out. Tony ended up going to prison for this. I managed to get off as the staff didn't name me. Typically, I never gave a second thought to what I was doing or its possible consequences.

I was still seeing Lesley, on and off, though our relationship was just as hard as ever. My paranoia had worsened and I was constantly plagued by destructive thoughts that ambushed me from nowhere. I was drinking more heavily. It began with two or three pints of an evening, then became half a dozen, which eventually became a dozen or more. The volume of alcohol consumed was proportional to the damage I would cause. A couple of pints and I would lay a few punches on some unsuspecting bloke. A dozen would see me going completely over the top, leaving my boot print on someone's bloodied, unconscious head. I was dangerous for two reasons. One, I didn't care who I fought and never considered whether I could beat them or not, and second, I had no sympathy for anyone. After I'd beaten someone to a pulp I didn't feel a thing – or at least not until the red mist had subsided, which took a very long time. Only then did I feel even a twinge of remorse.

One day when I was with Lesley she dropped the bombshell on me that she was pregnant. I was just 17 and deeply troubled; now I was going to be a dad. A father, me? This messed up kid? Would I change for my own child and try to put the past behind me once and for all? I was struggling to deal with myself, so I couldn't imagine how I would manage with a baby. Nevertheless, I decided I should move in with Lesley and give this a go. I left my mam and dad's and set up home as a so-called grown up.

My daughter was born in the April of 1984. I was on cloud nine. She was precious, cherished; I loved her more than anything. Once again my feelings were thrown into turmoil. I would look at myself in the mirror, see the person I'd become, and think I wasn't fit to have such a beautiful daughter. Voices haunted my mind, saying things like, "People like you don't deserve things like this..." This kind of self-pity gave me some degree of contentment. Misery was a part of me and, in a sense, I was comfortable with it. It was my comfort zone – the place I was familiar with. "You can't even look after yourself," the voice would say. "How can you look after your daughter, Swanny? You're a complete waste of space."

I tried my best to be good enough, but my past overwhelmed me. People had had enough of me – my parents, the police, society, it felt like. I was constantly in serious trouble. My brother Tony was hanging around with our gang more often and we would rampage through the streets of Loughborough. Gang fights were common place and people were having pint glasses smashed into their faces on a regular basis, all fuelled by alcohol. I came in front of magistrates many times and was either fined or told to do community service. I was remanded in custody regularly, but all of this failed to convince me to change my ways.

One time, when a man we knew wanted to get his hands on some firearms, we immediately knew of a house where some were being kept and could be stolen. We named our price and a deal was struck. Me, Tony and Roy took the job on. Tony did the breaking and entering while me and Roy waited outside, using a stolen car for a getaway vehicle. After a tense few minutes Tony came walking round the corner. He had a shotgun stuffed down each leg of his trousers and was walking stiff-legged, like Frankenstein. The sight of this caused me and Roy to burst out laughing. For a joke I leaned out of the window and told Tony to be careful, saying he was stupid to shove loaded guns down his trousers because they could go off. His face paled when I said this; it hadn't crossed his mind. Then, every time he got near the car we pulled off a little distance and then stopped again. Tony didn't see the funny side of our antics.

Some time after this incident Tony was arrested for a number of different crimes and the firearms were taken into consideration. He ended up receiving another prison sentence and was put away for it.

Meanwhile, I was father to a perfect, innocent little girl and busy trying to kid myself into believing life was good. It was a lie. Deep down I was full of darkness and insecurity. I lied to others, telling them that everything was great, but I didn't know who I was or where I was going. I vowed to exchange my terrible past for a brighter future and become a better person, but I failed Lesley and my little girl with my false promises. It wasn't long before the police were knocking on my door again – this time for something more serious. All I wanted to do was be with my baby girl, but instead I was hauled up before a judge. Within hours I would be on my way to a new home; one which consisted of three meals a day, scrubbing floors and fighting to survive – prison.

5
BROKEN PROMISES

As the judge passed sentence my heart sank into the depths of despair. I'd finally dug my own grave, like I always knew I would. I was overcome with feelings of utter worthlessness. The long list of misdemeanours I'd committed flashed before my eyes: endless brutality, muggings, robberies. But all these thoughts were superseded by a single thought: my little girl. All I could think about, as the judge told me what punishment I would receive, was how I'd have to leave my baby daughter and it was all my fault. I heard the man's words, but they didn't register. I had let down and disappointed Lesley. My mam and dad were genuinely saddened by this turn of events and I'd also let myself down – all my promises broken and ruined. I was on my way out of the lives of those I loved, to be locked away like an out of control animal.

Perhaps the harshest thing about receiving a custodial sentence is that, once sentence is passed, you are taken down immediately. There is a brutal disconnection of relationship with your loved ones as you are taken away. The journey to the Young Offenders Institute was one of the longest I'd ever experienced. The engine droned remorselessly in the background as though drowning out the sound of my former life. I desperately wanted to cry. I knew I needed to cry, in fact. It dawned on me that for years I had wanted to cry but never knew how. I wanted to know how it felt to be able to flush out all that pent up emotion instead of attempting, unsuccessfully, to bury it. But it never happened. Once again I put a lid on it. No matter how heavy going this next chapter of my life was, I would continue to deny my soul the relief of release.

The moment the judge passed sentence on me I was struck by the sinking sense that I had thrown away everything I cherished. I was about to be locked up and, although it wasn't a high security prison, it was a secure unit and I was being deprived of my freedom. I felt very isolated.

It was late when I arrived at the detention centre. The foreboding looking building was well-lit with harsh floodlights and protected by a double-walled fence, twenty feet high and topped with barbed wire. The gates were enormous and looked impenetrable. As you might imagine, iron bars interrupted the view from every window. This was my new home. I was scared rigid as two police officers escorted me into the building. Without ceremony I was processed immediately and asked a series of questions. I was instructed to address the prison guards as "Sir".

"You're nothing but a number now, boy. Do you hear me? Do you understand?" These words from a stony-faced prison guard slaughtered me, crushed my spirit. I'd only been there a few minutes and already I felt like cracking, overwhelmed by this new environment. But I knew I mustn't be weak. Yes, I felt defeated, but I knew I had to stay strong inside if I was going to survive here. My throat was dry, my voice quivering, "Yes, sir."

Next I was ordered to strip naked in a cold cubicle and given my new prison clothing. I felt a mixture of guilt, remorse and anger. I was disgusted with myself for allowing this to happen. Pleasantries over, I was taken to my cell and the thick metal door banged behind me, locks sliding across. This was it – I was alone; cut off from my family, friends, girlfriend and baby girl. There was nothing to do but lie in the darkness, overrun with shame, and reflect on my misery.

Mam and dad were suffering, just as I was. My life had been locked out of their reach for a long time now, not just by the detention centre. A week after I was sent away, Tony was jailed too. We had both ruined their lives through our selfish acts. Looking back, I can see this so clearly, but at the time the consequences of our actions never crossed our minds. Other people's feelings were irrelevant. It was all about us. Depression rocked both mam and dad as they tried to cope with the fallout of their wayward sons' lifestyles. All their weekends were taken up with visiting us in prison – me one week, Tony the next. It broke them; broke the family. I could see they were tormented by many sleepless nights spent worrying about us. They also blamed themselves for everything: "Why has this happened? What did we do wrong?" Whenever I spoke to them, though, I played the blame-shifting game. I never said to them, "It's not your fault, it's mine." I denied that any of this was my fault. "People always start on me for no reason, yet I get all the blame," I protested.

When you are on the outside, caught up in the whirlwind of life, you don't often stop to contemplate what you're doing. Life goes by. You just carry on. Besides, I didn't want to confront the turmoil that existed within me; instinctively I wanted to avoid the pain. But when you are bound by four brick walls, insulated from the outside world by an iron door, you are forced to reflect. I was forced to confront myself, perhaps for the first time. And though I didn't like what I found, it underlined one thing to me: I needed help. I knew I would never overcome my problems on my own. I had proven that conclusively. But what could I do? I couldn't find a way to admit my weakness and cry for help.

I'd stomached the crushing feelings of guilt from being weak, bullied and abused; for causing my mam and dad's pain. I ached with remorse over being an absent father, locked up night after night while my baby grew up. But I was still in fighting mode – fighting off emotions or fighting other inmates. Surely I still had to protect myself, didn't I? Otherwise the bullies could take control of me again. Show one chink in your armour in prison and it's goodbye.

Sharing life behind bars with a group of like-minded teenagers was a recipe for disaster. Every person had issues of one sort or another, due to a troubled past; everyone battling their inner demons. Here was a group of lads with very little self-worth, but at the same time bursting with aggression. We were all rebels, all living on our nerves and hostility was widespread. Often the hostility boiled over just after visiting time. When our families visited, we were confronted with our own guilt and shame. Seeing loved ones crying in every corner of the room ignited a self-anger that was hard to control. Frequently, on our way back to our rooms, someone would explode and all hell would break loose. It was a release; our way to handle the pressure.

Fighting inside was rampant. There was always something

kicking off. As a result I lost all my remission, so there was no possibility of me getting out early. Many times I was frogmarched away from some incident by the prison guards, hands restrained behind my back. They threw me into solitary – a small, concrete cell with no windows – and there I would stay for a few days to cool off until I was hauled before the governor to be punished further. Usually it meant a further loss of remission and being ordered to remain on the block for several days.

It was so boring in there. Days on end of nothingness passed, staring at the four walls while sitting on a chair made of cardboard. I either walked around my cell or just sat there while the clock ticked my sentence away. It wrecked me inside, but I still kept up the "don't care" façade.

Some prisons around that time had stable doors on the toilets. If you were in there longer than about thirty seconds the guards would kick the door open, whether you'd finished or not. This was just another way of stripping away your dignity. They didn't care in the slightest. I reckoned they enjoyed their jobs a little too much. They were aggressive and, more often than not, very willing to use violence to enforce the rules.

We were forced to participate in an incredibly hard physical training programme at the unit, which was clearly designed to wear us out, work off pent up emotions and, as much as possible, sap the desire to fight. Circuit training was popular. We were made to do bunny hops in their hundreds, followed by innumerable press-ups, followed by scores more bunny hops until we vomited.

Then there were the inspections to get through and military style drills on the parade ground. The regime was severe, but it was meant to be. Life here was supposed to be tough. As well as the physical training we would be put to work every day scrubbing the dormitories – with a toothbrush rather than a broom and mop sometimes, as a punishment. It didn't matter how well we followed the rules though, the guards would always find some excuse to give us a pasting.

At night, when all was silent, I would wrestle with my thoughts and emotions. I grieved the loss of my freedom. I indulged in self-pity. Despite this, my aggression grew thicker, like weeds in an untended garden, suffocating every other emotion. Being locked away was supposed to be teaching me a lesson, but instead it was fuelling my anger. It gave me another reason to hate the world. Prison was supposed to reform my character, but it didn't change my way of thinking at all. I had been excluded from normal life, but what was "normal"? To me, normality was taking what you wanted, causing destruction along the way, and damning the consequences. That was my normal.

* * *

All things pass and, in due course, I was released to resume my life. I had got it into my head that perhaps things would improve if I married Lesley. I thought that having a wife and a baby, having a proper home, would somehow change everything for the better. Maybe it would erase the past and write a new future? So Lesley and I married but, of course, I was wrong. It wasn't that simple. I was still the same person inside. Continual flare-ups rocked our world, igniting as easily as a match to petrol. I was kidding myself that life was good. I wasn't a whole person and the darkness inside continually overwhelmed me. If I went out for a drink with mates I would end up fighting. Every time I looked in the mirror I would despise myself and that led to more drinking to numb the pain and then more fighting.

Thanks to my dad I had started working at least. He had stuck his neck out for me and begged someone to give me a job at a local factory that made parts for trains and aeroplanes. I was a semi-skilled machine operator. It was a mind-numbingly boring job, doing the same tasks over and over again for eight hours. The other blokes kept telling me, "You should be glad for a job like this, son. They don't come up very often." Others said things that made me shudder, like, "I've been here for over twenty years and I've hated every minute of it."

"Brilliant," I'd reply, "now I know what I've got to look forward to for the rest of my life."

There was only one good thing about the job – there was a good gang of lads who worked there, including many of my close drinking mates. It was odd how we'd all ended up in the same factory. We had many good laughs together, but I acted the fool too often. Shamefully, I wasn't grateful that I had a job. I should have taken providing for my family much more seriously – especially as Lesley was now expecting our second child.

The day my son was born was such a perfect one for me. I was so pleased. Now I had one of each – who could ask for more? But Lesley and I continued to damage one another. We would argue over anything and everything. We both knew it wasn't working between us and we couldn't kid ourselves that things would be any better now with two kids than they were with one. I had never told Lesley the truth about my past, so how could our relationship ever be fixed? She didn't know who I really was. Instead of life getting better it continued as before. I carried on drinking and fighting, hanging out with the same lads and getting into all kinds of strife.

The police were never far from our door and I believed what

everyone said about me: I was a fool and a trouble-maker who'd sooner smash someone with a baseball bat than shake their hand. I called myself "a joke" and I truly believed it. Those people who wrote me off – the kids at school, the teachers, the police, judges, prison guards, blokes at work and many others – they were all right. I was a waste of space; no use to anyone.

6
WHAT IF'S

What if my brother hadn't gotten into so much trouble? Would I still have gone the same route? What if I hadn't been bullied? Would I have had the self-confidence to walk away from my abuser? What if I hadn't been sexually abused? What If I had walked away from so many fights instead of losing my temper and wading in? What if things were better at home? Could we have any kind of life together?

My life seemed to be defined by an endless string of what if's. What if, what if, what if... The questions pestered my brain until I thought it would haemorrhage. I desperately wanted them to stop. As a result, violence was always near the surface. It took next to nothing for some poor, unsuspecting soul to trigger the detonation. At one time I would start a fight with some verbal intimidation; nowadays I skipped the introduction and steamed in to finish the job before it had even started.

All of this took its toll. My heart was exhausted; I was drained of every good emotion. Before I was exposed to the cruelty of the world I had been contented with my life. Now I had sunk into a deep depression. And the saddest part is, I didn't even know I was depressed. I knew I was angry – irritated by people, annoyed at the slightest thing, sick of my self-destructive thoughts, but I couldn't put a label on it. The years of mental, physical and sexual abuse had driven me deep into myself. Years of bitterness, hurt, anger and violence were keeping me locked up there.

I hardly ate anything during this period of my life. I drank to excess and filled myself up on beer, suppressing my appetite with fags. I hadn't had any proper food, like my mam used to make, for a long time. I wasn't sleeping either. I'd go to bed exhausted, hoping to rest, but in between brief snatches of sleep I spent the majority of time reliving my past. On top of this I suffered regular anxiety attacks. I was constantly agitated, nervous and uneasy. On the outside I was a confident, outgoing, entertainer at best and, at worst, a heavy drinking, violent idiot who might kill someone one day if he wasn't careful. On the inside, I was a dead man walking. I always struggled to smile. People constantly asked me what was wrong or issued a glib, "Cheer up son, it may never happen." It took every bit of strength I had to maintain the cocky front that everything was fine. I was a long way from fine. Many times I wanted to break down and cry; to shout out and tell everyone what I'd been through and how it had affected me. But there were no tears and no confession.

* * *

The arguments at home were never ending. It wasn't healthy for any of us, especially not the kids. I turned things over and over in my mind and then, one day came to a heartrending decision.

I was up early one morning. Lesley and the kids were still in bed. I sat staring out of the patio window, gripping a mug of hot tea for comfort. I rubbed my head, searching for answers. I had been telling myself for a while that the best thing I could do for this family was to leave, walk away. I was no good for any of them. I was afraid that the constant strife would destroy the kids' lives. I was torn between keeping the family together – if you could call it that – giving the kids a mam and dad at least – and removing myself to end everyone's suffering.

It ripped me apart. How could I think of leaving my kids? I loved them dearly. How could I pack my gear up and walk away from the best things in my life? They were everything to me; my reason for living. Yet our house wasn't a home; it was just an address we all happened to live at.

I took a sip of my tea but it was hard to swallow. My throat closed up with emotion. If I decided to do this, I knew there was no return. Once I opened that door and walked away, that would be it. I'd be saying goodbye to their confused faces, wondering where and why daddy was going. My emotions were raw. I wanted to cry, but I was afraid that if I started I would never stop.

Somehow, my mind was made up that today must not end like so many days before; something different had to happen. I was ill and emaciated. Lesley and I had lived in a toxic relationship for too long. What we had together fuelled my anger and fed my depression. I had to go. I had to say goodbye. Although I hated the expected consequences of leaving my kids, in the end I felt it would be better for them if I wasn't there. The decision cut me in two, but the dye was cast. I didn't want my kids to have to live in this pressure cooker any longer.

The separation was tough and leaving my children was

heart-breaking. I was a screwed up 26-year-old when I took the decision to walk away. Suddenly I was back at mam and dad's house. I know they could have done without it. Dad wasn't a good sleeper himself and always had to be up early for work. Me rolling in at all hours smashed out of my head didn't go down well.

At the same time I was finding it hard to hold down my dead-end job. It was my own fault. I had played the fool one too many times. When hard times hit, my name was top of the list of people to make redundant. I seemed to ruin everything I touched. After losing my job I disappeared into myself for a few months and drank even more heavily. The violence went hand in hand with the drinking, forming a brutal loop of behaviour I couldn't escape from. The first thing I'd do every morning when I woke up was have a drink. Morning, noon and night I had a bottle to my lips. I was well-oiled by ten in the morning. Yet, part of me knew I couldn't just drink myself into a coma each day, so I looked for ways to break free.

A brief respite and a helping hand came from Jimmy Molloy, the dad of my mates, Andy and Brian. I was very close to Jimmy. I loved him so much. Jimmy had a window cleaning round. He eventually gave me some of his round so that I could begin to build up my own – for which I was very grateful.

It was physically demanding work, up and down the ladders all day. Especially if I was dragging myself out of bed after a heavy drinking night or if I was battered and bruised from a fight. It was good to be working, but even window cleaning had the ability to make me angry. If it was raining outside that meant I couldn't work. I'd watch the weather report every evening and if they mentioned rain I'd go ballistic!

As soon as I'd finished my window cleaning round, I always went round to see my kids. Every second of the day I looked forward to seeing them. They were my whole reason for living. I explained to them from day one that I had left their mother, not them, and stressed that none of this was their fault in any way. I tried to save them blaming themselves. The guilt would tear me in two. I was happy they weren't having to hear their mam and dad argue all the time, but miserable because we weren't all living under the same roof. They were growing up fast and I wanted to be a part of their lives. I just missed them so much.

Being apart from my kids was the toughest fight I'd ever known. But in some strange way it became a catalyst for me. It ignited a small spark within me – a resolve that somehow I must change my life. It was only small, but it was a start. I dreamed of a better life for us. I had a vision that one day, possibly, I could live free from the pain of the past; that I'd be able to sleep and have dreams in which I didn't see the faces of my bullies or my abuser; that I'd wake without a heavy heart; that things could be "normal".

Although I hadn't changed a great deal, I knew there had to be more to life than this. There just had to be. I'd been searching for the missing jigsaw piece for what felt like forever. Exactly what it was, I didn't exactly know, but I was certain that there must be something I was missing. I teetered on the precipice between despair and hope.

7

A GAP IN THE CLOUDS

The passage of time and prolonged separation had taken its course. Lesley and I were now divorced. Things just didn't work when we were together. We had no future. We both knew it, probably from the beginning; it just took us both a long time to admit it. So what now?

The day started like any other. I woke up feeling rough, needing a drink, though I still reeked of the booze I'd had the night before. I didn't know it, but this day would mark a new chapter in my life – one of renewed hope. No matter what any person has been through and however they may have been intimidated, bullied, even abused, I believe that deep inside there is still treasure to be found somewhere. Sometimes it just takes a special kind of person to help us find it.

For the last two days it had been raining, so I hadn't got much work done. Today the sky was clear, so I could earn a bit of cash. Though my head was still banging, I knew that if I wanted to go out for a drink that evening, it had to be done. I didn't earn loads that day, but it was enough for a few drinks and a bag of chips on the way home.

Later, I phoned a mate and arranged to go out. I was showered, dressed and on my way out like so many other nights, ready to numb the pain inside. I kidded myself that I was socialising; a few drinks with people I enjoyed being with. But it was never like that. I would drink as much as I could. Then, when I'd reached my absolute maximum, I'd drink some more. If I was still standing after that, I'd have one more for the road. I couldn't face going home alone unless I was smashed and I'd usually caused some aggravation before I'd left. I'd wake up the next morning wondering how I'd got home and why my face had been punched inside out. Usually I would find out what had happened later from a mate.

This night was going like clockwork so far. We'd already had enough to drink and I expected this night to end like any other. Then my mate spotted a couple of girls on the other side of the pub and wanted me to go over with him to start a conversation. We made our way over. I'd seen one of the girls – the one I liked – around the Shelthorpe area from time to time. Normally I would never have made the first move to speak, but with a few beers inside me I thought, why not?

"Hello, what's your name then?" I asked, the drink giving me a false self-confidence. I looked at her and couldn't help grinning like an idiot. She looked stunning. My heart raced and I felt nervous – that rush of adrenalin you feel when you really like someone. I'd never known anything like it.

"My name's Rachel, what's yours?"

"Graham," I said, wondering if my eagerness was apparent. I suddenly hoped I wasn't slurring my words because I was so gobsmacked by this woman.

"Graham what?"

"Swann," I said. "Just call me Swanny, everybody else does. Do you want a drink?"

The remainder of that evening was filled with a few drinks and a lot of laughter. Me and Rachel spoke for hours. It felt as though I had known her forever. It was like we were the only ones in the pub and time flew by. It was the best night I'd had in years. As closing time was called, I asked Rachel if I could see her again and hoped she'd say yes. I really liked her and it took a lot for me to work myself up to ask the question. She took a pen and a bit of paper out of her bag and scribbled down her phone number. "Call me tomorrow, Swanny," she said before we said our goodbyes.

That night I couldn't sleep. I thought about Rachel constantly and relived the evening. I remembered how she'd looked at me while we were talking, smiling and laughing. Her smile was infectious and her eyes ... they sparkled like I'd never seen before. I was hooked.

Morning came around quickly. I was awake at the crack of dawn and a quick glance outside revealed the makings of a beautiful day. I crept downstairs and made myself a drink, still thinking about Rachel. I sat on the back doorstep, sipping my tea. It was the first day I'd known in decades where I felt I had something to look forward to. Later I got out to work and, for once, window cleaning didn't feel like such a chore. The sun was out and I'd met the most beautiful woman. Plus, she'd given me her phone number. Result!

It was a strange day too though, to be truthful. Mostly I felt happy, fortunate to have met Rachel and pleased that she wanted to see me again. But that old, familiar part of me nagged with disturbing thoughts. "It'll all go wrong … it always does … nothing good ever lasts…" I tried to reason with myself; I hadn't even spoken to Rachel yet. Surely this was just my paranoia kicking in.

I finished my round at 5.00pm and felt shattered. It was the mind games rather than the work that had worn me out. An entire day of, "She likes me, she likes me not" had driven me to distraction. I rushed home, had some tea, showered, then plucked up the courage to give her a call. I was nervous. I must have picked up the phone a dozen times, dialled her number and put the receiver down before it rang. Eventually I went through with it.

"Hello?" a voice answered.

"Hello, is that Rachel?" My voice quaked. I wasn't confident with women at the best of times and less so without a drink inside me.

"Hi, is that Swanny?" Rachel replied.

Instantly my rejection radar was up. I detected a subtle but different tone in her voice. Here it was … what I'd expected all day … things were about to go wrong again.

"What's up, Rachel?" I asked tentatively.

"Can you do me a favour and come round my house?" Rachel asked. "I want to talk to you face to face."

"Yeah, I'll be there as soon as I can."

The journey to Rachel's house was riddled with thoughts of doubt and disappointment. I prepared myself for the worst. I knew it was coming. My heart was pounding as I knocked on her door. Her face looked serious when she opened it and I just knew – that was it.

"Come in, Swanny. I want to ask you a few things."

We walked through to her kitchen and sat down. I felt like I was being questioned by the serious crime squad. Rachel had been doing her homework that day and the things she was hearing from others weren't good. She didn't mince her words.

"Right, Swanny," she said. "I've been told you've been to prison, is that true?"

I wasn't going to lie, there was no point. I had nothing to gain by it and I could tell from her face that she knew all about it anyway.

"Yeah," I answered with a nervous smile.

"What for?" Her reply was sharp. There were no smiles.

"Fighting."

"Do you break into houses?"

"No, never." She was making me more nervous by the minute.

"I've been told by lots of people to keep well away from you Swanny. People say you're bad news and wherever you go, trouble isn't far behind."

"Don't believe everything you hear, Rachel," I pleaded. "I'm not that bad. It's just that I get a bit hot-headed when I've had too much to drink." I tried to explain things as best as I could. I didn't want her to be put off. I really liked her. I knew where she was coming from though and I understood why she was being cautious. She had a lot to lose. Rachel had already been through one relationship that turned out to be violent. The last thing she needed was to walk straight into another. She had two lovely little girls herself who needed her protection, so she needed to check me out. I respected her for that.

Rachel pulled no punches and fired questions at me for the next couple of hours. Each time I told her the truth. And despite being under interrogation, I felt happy in her presence. Rachel made me feel safe – something I hadn't felt for as long as I could remember. Instinctively I knew that something could grow between the two of us, if it was allowed to. The only problem was, how could I explain to her about the darkness I still carried inside? How could I articulate the pain that had gripped me since I was a 10-year old little boy? It seemed an impossible mountain to climb.

Rachel decided to give it a go with me. She thought I was worth the risk. She said that behind all my tattoos she could see a really nice person. "You don't have to control your life with your fists," she told me. "You should use your heart. It's love that makes the world go round, Swanny."

Was my life going to change? Was I going to start getting a bit of what I'd missed out on for so long? I really hoped so. I wanted things to be different. Up until meeting Rachel my life had been one long struggle. It was true what she said, trouble had walked hand-in-hand with me. Was it possible to break free from this destructive cycle?

* * *

The months ticked by and I took the window cleaning business more seriously. I bought myself a van and had a logo put on each side to advertise my service. I was actually making a living and conducting my work life like a normal person. Life had taken a step in the right direction now that Rachel was part of it. But I was far from perfect. Inside, anger still simmered and could easily be provoked, like flipping a coin. One minute I was heads, the next tails. Nevertheless, despite my unpredictability, Rachel continued to see the good in me and we eventually moved in together. We were a good match for each other and our relationship was moving in the right direction.

Shortly, we moved to a new area. The house we got was a bit of a mess, but we worked on it together and put our own stamp on it. We loved each other and that was reflected in the house. It became more than just an address, it was a home – something that had eluded me for so long. Being in a loving, stable relationship for the first time was breath taking. I loved Rachel's girls and she welcomed my kids to stay over, which they did all the time. All the kids got on with each other brilliantly and that took the pressure off us both. We were a family. The love we needed to make this a success blossomed and grew.

Rachel and I grew ever closer. Each day I loved her more than the last and the feeling was mutual. The kids were fine and our home was great. Work was busy and it was paying the bills and putting food on the table. But something still jarred. One day I realised: I'm not happy doing this – it's just not me. Rachel is no fool and she could see I was restless. She knew I had ghosts in my past that I wasn't talking about, though she never pressed me to speak about it.

One evening though, when the kids were in bed, she asked me, "What do you really want out of life?" My instinct was to respond with, "I just want to be happy." But how could I say that? It would have given her completely the wrong impression. What I meant was, I was tired of living in the past; tired of the depression and sleepless nights. But I wasn't ready to share the "why" with her. Instead, I sat quietly for a while, processing my thoughts. Then I recalled my childhood conversation with my Granddad. "Don't laugh," I said. "But since I was a little boy, I've always wanted to be a tattooist, because of my Granddad." I waited for her to burst out laughing, but it didn't happen. She just lovingly looked me in the eyes and said, "Be one then!" I knew she genuinely meant it.

I appreciated her love and her supportive attitude, but my rejection self-defence mechanism kicked in immediately. "What? How can someone like me become a tattooist?" I objected. "Anyway, it was just a thought I had once; I never took it seriously." Then I remembered an inspiring quote I'd once heard: If you know why you want something, you will find the how. Rachel and I talked about it at length and she encouraged me to go for it — to start doing something I could be passionate about.

Decision made, I went all out to get into the tattooing business. I needed to keep up the window cleaning round to pay the bills and provide for the family, but after work I would rush home, grab some food, then drive over to Leicester where I did my training. It was hard going, but after months of working my guts out and travelling backwards and forwards, my dream became a reality. I was a qualified tattooist and I was able to start my own business in Shelthorpe.

* * *

In time, Rachel and I were married. It was a lovely day for both of us, but I was still my old insecure self. I refused to give a speech at the reception. I was so frightened of mixing up my words and looking like an idiot.

What followed, however, were some great times — holidays away as a family, seeing the kids grow up and making our home just the way we wanted it to be. There were lots of funny moments to be had chatting with clients in the tattoo studio and we made some great friends along the way. Life was good. We made the best of it. Then, in 1996, we decided to have our own baby together. I was so proud of Rachel the day our little boy was born. All our kids were special to us and we both loved all of them to bits. But having our own son was the icing on the cake and completed our family.

The presence of genuine love in the context of a real family brought about a change in me. The anger began to subside, bit by bit. What I found odd was the fact that the anger wasn't replaced by peace; it was replaced by sadness and depression. Instead of feeling a lift in my spirits, I felt low, thinking about how much of life I'd missed out on. Deep down my core beliefs had not changed. I still had that in-built script that said, "I don't deserve to be happy." I wanted so much to tell Rachel about my past; to explain about the bullying, the sexual abuse. But I always stopped short of doing it.

Viewed from the outside my life looked good. I had the woman of my dreams, five great healthy kids, a lovely home (not just a house), a reliable car and, eventually, a tattooing business that would give us a good living, holidays and some of the nice things in life. But inside me it was a different story. I was unable to get over my secret past. It was always there to haunt me and rob me of enjoying all these good things. The only way out of this nightmare was, I thought, to drink myself into oblivion. If I was drunk, then at least I would sleep and have some respite from my persecuted thoughts.

One of the side effects of my troubled childhood was that I'd never go into our house if there was no one home. I suppose it stemmed from the time when I was about 12 and I heard that Tony had run away from the children's home. He went missing for several weeks and the police were looking for him everywhere. My mam and dad were worried sick and didn't know whether he was dead or alive. Unbeknown to us, Tony had been hiding in the loft of our house and one day, when I walked in alone, he jumped down and frightened me to death. From that day on I had an irrational fear of entering an empty house. I had carried this for years.

If I'd finished work for the day and was ready to go home I would phone Rachel to see where she was. She might say, "I'm shopping Swanny" or "I'm at my mums." Perfectly normal things, but they would cause a chill to run through my body. Not being able to face the empty house I'd say, "Come home now then babes," and try to persuade her to go home. Because she loved me Rachel was always kind enough to stop what she was doing and come home. She never questioned why I was the way I was, she just went along with it, guessing I had some secret reason for it.

Sometimes she would find me sitting on the doorstep, but sometimes I'd retreated to the pub. If I thought she was taking too long, I'd go down to my local. Then I'd get a taste for the beer and by the time Rachel was home she'd have to phone me to ask where I was. Too many times I said, "I'm down the pub; I'll be home after this one" and Rachel knew full well that the next time she'd see me I'd be completely hammered.

The next day when reality kicked in, I'd realise I'd let the drink beat me again. I was ashamed to let Rachel down, something I hated doing, and ashamed that the kids had seen me paralytic one more time. Ultimately, the drink never did help. Still, in the dead of night, the lost boy would come and visit me, trying to persuade me to keep all of this locked up inside when I wanted so badly to let it all out.

All I wanted was to tell Rachel the truth. How could I find a way?

8

LIGHT BREAKS THROUGH

Since the age of 10 I had lived wearing many disguises. Each new disguise overlaid the previous ones in a dark confusion. I could appear happy when I wanted to, nod in the right places, smile when the occasion called for it, laugh at the right times. But underneath all those phony performances I was still the lost boy trapped in an adult's body, screaming to get out. The lies I believed about myself convinced me I'd never be healed of the past; never be a whole person.

Though life had improved dramatically and I had much to be grateful for, I was still an emotional prisoner. I wanted nothing more than to spill my guts and let the ugly truth out – to tell the person I loved most what I had been through. But at the same time, the thought of doing so terrified me. It meant that, for the first time ever, I'd have to let my guard down and become completely vulnerable – something I had trained myself not to do. Plus, it was hard enough coping with the truth myself; how would I cope with someone else knowing my inner torment?

Scared to let go, I decided to suffer in silence and carry on the act.

I'd kept up this pretence for more than 30 years now. Imagine playing the part of one person for 30 years, all the while being a completely different person inside. That was me. I was an actor in a long-running soap opera I'd never agreed to sign up to. Thirty Christmases starved of happiness, my mind savaged by the indignity of being thrashed, half-naked by my bullies and the embarrassment of being sexually abused. Thirty years living as a twofold-person with all the emotional fallout that caused. Heads or tails? Confusion, confusion, confusion.

In the summer of 2006, however, another chance meeting caused a new twist in my journey. I have a good friend called Steve, a great sax player who makes the instrument sing and plays with such sincerity that it never fails to bring a smile to your face. Steve's sister, Louise, married an American called Tyler and they lived in Florida for a while, but in 2006 they moved back to the UK. Had they not, my life might have turned out very differently.

I was introduced to Tyler while I was hanging out with Steve one day. He was an easy-going, gentle guy and I took to him instantly. I noticed that he seemed to be a very peaceful person. I thought maybe this was an American thing; perhaps everyone from Florida was this laid back? We bumped into each other frequently over coming months and became friends. One day I asked him if he'd like to go out for a pint. "That would be great, buddy!" he said, sounding pleased.

Over a couple of pints at a local pub Tyler told me how much he loved America and explained how he'd worked there as both a fire-fighter and a paramedic. He also mentioned that he'd left just a few years before qualifying for his pension, leaving it all behind to come to England. I was amazed. I couldn't understand the logic behind his decision. "Have you lost the plot?" I asked, half laughing. "Why would anyone throw all that away to come and live in Loughborough?" (I'm not saying there is anything wrong with Loughborough, by the way, it's a great place – but Florida?) Tyler had given up a fantastic career and a guaranteed pension. I wanted to know why.

He confirmed with a grin that he hadn't, in fact, "lost the plot".

"Well what made you come over from America and leave a job you loved?" I asked. "You gave it all up and missed out on a great pension too. Plus, you left the lovely sunshine there for the woeful weather of Loughborough. Why?"

"God told me to," he replied matter-of-factly.

I almost choked on my beer. He'd said it like it was the most natural thing in the world.

"What are you on about?" I said, laughing in his face. I thought the cheese had fallen off his cracker. "You mean your instincts told you to?"

"No buddy, I mean God told me to."

I persisted with my logical reasoning. "How can God talk to you? You mean your instincts."

"Yeah, if you like, buddy, my instincts," he replied calmly.

He went on to explain that he was a Christian. He'd given up his great job and pension to come to Loughborough because, apparently, "God had told him to". I thought he was completely nuts.

But despite what I saw as Tyler's crackpot beliefs, our friendship deepened. "Each to their own," I thought. Tyler and

Louise would often come round to our house for meals. We had some lovely times together and would talk for hours. They told us all about their life in America and both Rachel and I loved every second of their company.

Louise is a softly spoken, gentle girl. She'd had a number of health issues over the years and as a result was unable to have children of her own. One day, as we sat together eating a lovely meal Rachel had made, Tyler and Louise told us about the time when God "put it on their hearts" to adopt a child from China. They said that God had spoken to both of them, separately, whilst they were both at work. When they eventually got home and spoke to each other about it, they were amazed how God had told them the same thing. In due course, they did go to China and came back with a little daughter who they named Jada. Jada was 5 years old when they moved to England. She was a beautiful little girl with long black hair and a cute American accent. Tyler and Louise both gave God all the credit for arranging for them to be the parents of this little girl. Rachel and I were amazed by what they were telling us, even if we didn't really understand it. We noticed that not once did they ever complain about the fact that they couldn't have their own child naturally – they just thanked God for their blessings.

As time went on, I listened to Tyler speak about God on many occasions. It wasn't for me, but I respected who he was and what he believed in. He talked very openly about his relationship with Jesus. I admired him for that and noticed the amount of love and compassion he had for anyone he met. All this was still odd to me, but I didn't judge him for what he obviously sincerely believed.

One day we were chatting over a cup of tea, as we'd done

many times before, and suddenly the conversation headed off into unknown territory. Tyler sipped his tea and then looked me in the eye. He told me that God had shown him that I was hurting deep within. But God wanted me to know that He loved and cared for me. I was completely taken aback. After a couple of seconds of awkward silence, I denied that there was anything wrong, of course, as was my habit. But as Tyler spoke the words, they rang true. Maybe the God that I had prayed to all those years ago actually existed. But if He did, why would He care about me?

Tyler's words stayed with me. It was like the time when Rachel first told me she loved me – I just couldn't get those words out of my head for weeks. "Get a grip, Swanny, and don't be soft!" I chided myself. "Don't you dare fall for all this rubbish. You've been strong. You've got this far without God. Don't give up now!" But for all that, I knew that deep down I was kidding myself. I was hurting and, yes, I was powerless to do anything about it. I wasn't strong at all – far from it. But I had built my barricade and maintained it for years. No one was going to be allowed into my private space – especially not God!

The next time the four of us got together for a meal I fired a string of questions at Tyler and Louise. They seemed very genuine people. I wanted to know whether any of this God-stuff was really real or they were just deluded. Nice, but deluded.

"So what happens when I die," I wanted to know. "I'm not that bad a person; I've never killed anyone. Do I go to heaven or hell?"

Louise did her best to explain. "No one goes to heaven when they die because of the good things they've done in life, Swanny," she said. "It's not about being good or bad. You don't get to heaven on brownie points. The Bible says that Christ shows us the way. It says that Jesus is the way, the truth and the life."

I tried to take in all she was saying.

"That doesn't mean it's difficult to become a Christian," she continued. "But believing in Him is the way you do it, because Jesus alone died for our sins to make us right before God. When we believe this, we're set free inside. We have eternal life and we can also live life to the full on earth through Christ. We can have peace, knowing that God loves us."

She may as well have been speaking Russian. I didn't understand how any of this could happen. Over coming weeks I had lots more questions for Tyler over cups of tea. "Why don't you just come to church with me one week, Swanny?" he eventually said. I looked at him as though he'd just fallen out of the sky. "Thanks, but no thanks," I said emphatically. "I've been to church before – funerals and weddings, you know – it was boring; it did my head in." Tyler's invitation took me back to when I was a very small boy. I remembered my mam taking me to church. I couldn't remember why or what for, but the memory had stayed with me.

The next few weeks were spent battling many emotions. I visited places inside me that I hadn't been for a long time, as well as all the regular haunts. I went through some agonising days, feelings flooding through me, overwhelming me, confusion swirling around my head. I was in utter turmoil. Over the years Rachel had known that something was wrong with me. The way I would react to situations and flip at the slightest thing were dead giveaways. The slightest wrong look or offhand comment and I would be off my head with rage. It wasn't normal behaviour. I knew it; Rachel knew it. Now it seemed like Tyler knew it too. To tell the truth, I was sick and tired of being sick and tired. Was it time to go to church?

The next time I saw Tyler I told him I'd been thinking a lot about what he'd been saying and, if the offer was still on, I'd like to go to church with him. I couldn't believe I was saying it.

"That'd be great, buddy," he smiled. "I'll pick you up this Sunday."

"Okay, see you then," I replied, all the while thinking, "What have I done?" I had just asked Tyler if I could go to church with him. Church! People like me didn't go to church. But something strange was happening inside me. I couldn't explain what was going on. All I knew was that I'd lived in a prison without bars for too long and it was time – my time – to break free, once and for all.

The remainder of that week was riddled with doubts. I was in two minds; heads I went, tails I didn't. But when Sunday came around I decided to go through with it. As I walked into church with Tyler I felt ridiculously anxious. I didn't know what to expect, but I guessed my appearance would be enough to put most people off. I have tattoos all over my head, in my ears, around my throat – in fact, my whole body is covered. What would people think of me? To my surprise, everyone was really nice. The church had a friendly, welcoming feeling and above all I didn't feel as though people were judging me. So far, I actually liked it. That is, until what happened next.

People stood up and started singing. They were singing about how God came first in their life, above everything else. "You've got to be joking," I thought to myself. "There's no way I'm going to stand up and sing this stuff. God doesn't come first in my life, Rachel and the kids do." Right then I made my mind up: I didn't like this and I wasn't coming back!

After the singing, the pastor, Paul Garner, got up to speak for a while. His words penetrated my heart. It was as though someone had told him all about my life and I felt as though he was speaking directly to me. He spoke with authority; his words rang with truth. I'd learnt over the years to spot when someone was being genuine and I saw in him the same authenticity I saw in Rachel and Tyler.

When the service was over, we hung around for a cup of tea and a chat. I really liked the people there – I just wasn't keen on the God bit. Tyler and Louise asked me how I felt about it all. I said I didn't know, but one thing was for sure, it was very lively and I certainly didn't expect that.

All the following week church was on my mind and I had lots of questions. Was there really a God out there? Was He alive and real, like my friends said He was? Did God love me like the Bible says? Could God heal me from my past? Could He really put right all the pain, the violence, the alcohol? So far nothing had been able to help me. First Tyler and then Paul had spoken about being "born again". What did that even mean? I wanted to understand more. Next time Tyler came round for a cup of tea I had more questions for him.

Tyler explained that human beings are part flesh and part spirit. We are born "in the flesh" from our parents, but we also have an eternal spirit, implanted in us by our Father in heaven, who is called God the Father. Each of us is born in a sinful state, separated from God the Father and unable to have a relationship with Him. But through His Son, Jesus, who paid the price for our sins on the cross, we can have our relationship with God restored. If we confess our belief in Jesus and believe in our heart that He died for us and rose again into life, then our spirit will come alive and we will be "born again" into a new life. Added to that, the Holy Spirit will come to live in us and give us strength. The Holy Spirit, Tyler told me, is like our doctor, our counsellor. He can relieve us of all the heavy burdens that have weighed us down all our lives.

All this was mind blowing to me. My head was spinning with it. I'd already had several weeks of pure bewilderment and now Tyler was telling me this.

"So, who's the Holy Spirit?" I asked.

Tyler tried to explain the best way he could to help me understand – that God is three persons in one: God the Father, God the Son and God the Holy Spirit. God became a man in Jesus so that He could die for our sins. Jesus rose from the dead to offer salvation to all people through spiritual renewal and re-birth. When Jesus ascended into heaven, His physical presence left the earth, but He promised to send the Holy Spirit so that His spiritual presence would be available to those who believed in Him. This new life is a gift from God – there is nothing we can do to earn it. The Holy Spirit is a wonderful friend, guide, counsellor and teacher. He isn't someone to be afraid of; He's all good. He doesn't replace Jesus, but He gives us a hunger to want Jesus at the centre of our lives.

I listened to all he had to say. I wasn't sure I understood it all. Tyler explained that this is where the issue of faith comes in.

"But what is faith?" I asked, posing another huge theological question.

"Faith is believing in something we can't see with human eyes," Tyler replied. "It's like a feeling of knowing, a hope, being sure of something in our heart."

He went on to explain that, in reality, we are not human beings capable of having a spiritual experience, but rather spiritual beings having a human experience. God made the real essence of each of us – our spirit. Nothing in life will ever satisfy us until we find our true home in Him.

As Tyler spoke, I felt a warmth come over me. It is hard to explain how that felt. Perhaps all I can say is that truth was penetrating my heart. One thing I knew for sure: nothing in life had ever satisfied me; I'd tried the lot and nothing had taken away my pain. Even my current happiness with Rachel and the kids wasn't making me a completely whole person. I knew there must be something more.

Some reading this may think, "He's the one who's lost the plot now and fallen for some phony religion." It wasn't like that. I was beginning to see clearly for the first time in my life. Though I was as sceptical as the next person, probably more so, somehow God was beginning to break into my well-defended fortress.

By the time the weekend came around I was looking forward to visiting the church again. I asked Rachel if she would come with me. She did, but when we got back home she told me she felt like a hypocrite and wouldn't come again. I understood. The following week I went alone. That Sunday, as pastor Paul was preaching, a wave of peace washed over me. I began to cry, but it felt okay to do so because at the same time I felt an overwhelming sense of real love enveloping me. It was amazing. I knew then, in my heart, that God was really alive. He was real and He wanted to be a part of my life. It was as though He was knocking on the door of my heart, but He couldn't just walk in unless I invited Him to do so.

So there and then, through all the tears and swirling emotions,

I asked God to come into my life. I asked Him to forgive me for all the things I'd done wrong and to help me with the problems I'd carried with me for so many years. More waves of overwhelming love swept over me and I knew... I was free at last. The love of God pushed back the blackness that had held me captive for so long. He drew me out of that darkness and into the light. In that moment He changed me. I was no longer that 10-year-old boy who'd been viciously bullied and sexually abused. I was finally free of the bars. All I could do was let the tears flow and say over and over again, "Thank you, God."

A different man returned home that day. I explained to Rachel that I'd become a Christian. She said she was pleased for me; whatever made me happy was okay with her. But she made it clear that it wasn't for her. I desperately wanted her to feel what I was feeling. I knew that she needed saving, like every other lost soul does. But I had to respect her decision. I knew though, that if God wanted a relationship with someone like me, then He wanted one with Rachel too. I hoped it was just a matter of time before it happened.

To say I felt different would be a massive understatement. I sat at home having a cup of tea with Rachel and I couldn't believe the change that had taken place inside me. I can barely find the words to describe it. I had let God into my life and the weight had been lifted from my shoulders. Life would never be the same again.

Then I heard a voice speak to me.

A long time ago a voice had begged me to keep quiet, to keep the secret, to not let it out and make myself vulnerable. Now a different voice said, "Tell Rachel the truth, Swanny." Whereas the previous voice brought with it fear and anxiety, this voice brought peace, a sense of love; somehow I knew everything was going to be okay.

"Rachel," I said. "I need to tell you something and I need you to listen. It's a long story."

PART TWO: RE-WRITING THE PAST

9

LIVING IN THE MOMENT

What God had done in my life was truly amazing. It was amazing that He wanted to touch my dark-as-pitch heart; to be a part of my life and deliver me from my misery. Despite my anger and the countless acts of violence I had committed; despite the rage I had inflicted on so many innocent people, He loved me and wanted to forgive me. I had been in utter emotional confusion for years, but here was a God who brought order where there was previously chaos. The Bible says, "God is not a God of confusion, but of peace" (1 Corinthians 14:33 ESV).

I used to be afraid to look inside myself, scared of what I might find. I hardly knew the true me at all. I didn't believe there could be anything good in me. But God came in and transformed me from the inside out. I was always looking for external things to bring me peace and happiness. Jesus showed me that we can find inner peace through Him. I used to think maybe I'd be happy if I achieved certain things in life, like going on exotic holidays or owning expensive cars. But as Jesus said, "What do you benefit if you gain the whole world but lose your own soul?" (Matthew 16:26 NLT). I came to realise, there is nothing wrong with material possessions, but they can't satisfy your soul; they will always leave you feeling hollow. We can't satisfy a longing that only God can fill.

After that special day when God touched me I began to rapidly change. God showed me that, just like me, the world was full of broken people, each struggling with their own pain and insecurities. We live in a hurting, disordered world. Yet, God is able to transform it by transforming us. Though at this point I may still have been a bit broken and rough round the edges, God showed me that I could still let others know how He could touch their lives. He birthed a new-found compassion in me. It was like discovering the missing piece to a jigsaw. Whereas before I felt no empathy for anyone, now I looked at others with new eyes.

I felt so much lighter; it was amazing. The knot in my stomach had been untied. The chains I'd been wrapped up in for so many years had been unravelled. I was released from my old way of life and shown a new one. I no longer felt that I had to fight the world. I'd been released from the prison without bars. Things seemed to move very fast for me. From that day, it was like God was working overtime, giving me a crash course in spiritual things. This isn't the same for everyone, I've found out. He works with us all differently, at our own pace. He has patience and will push us a little to encourage us, but it's always with guidance and love.

I was very aware that I was only on day one of this new journey. All my problems didn't disappear miraculously overnight. But I knew it was definitely a new beginning. I was in no doubt that God had set in motion the healing process I'd longed for. I knew that He couldn't just wipe my memories of the past, but He was taking away the pain and repairing me bit by bit like a Master Craftsman.

For many years I had struggled with negative, self-defeating thoughts. This tide of negativity didn't just turn off like flicking a switch. My mind was my battle ground and some days things were really tough. Some days still are. But back then, the more I nurtured negative thoughts about my past, the more they would self-seed. Every seed of negativity I allowed to take root, quickly grew into something the size of an oak tree. I never stopped to think that I might be in a spiritual battle, I just assumed it was all down to my mind. But every time I focused on God – the God of peace who wanted to bring His order into my chaos – the negativity subsided. As the saying goes, if you fall down seven times, then get up eight.

I was changing, day by day, and I wasn't the only one who was noticing it. Rachel had seen a huge transformation in me. Others began to comment that I seemed so much calmer. They'd always felt as though they needed to walk on eggshells around me; now I was different. Rachel told me later that often she would just lie in bed and gaze at me sleeping peacefully. You'll recall that this was something I could never do; I never slept well, tossing and turning all night as I battled with my thoughts and fears. God helped me overcome that. He also helped me overcome my fear of being alone in the house. I began coming home, even if no one else was around.

Rachel had noticed all of this. In a matter of weeks she found herself living with a completely different man. The change in me touched her heart. She too had her issues in life, things that needed resolving, so she began looking for answers. In response to her queries I would tell her about Jesus, answering as best as I could. It wasn't long before she started coming to church with me and, by the grace of God, had a faith of her own.

The day Rachel invited God into her life was such an emotional one. I couldn't believe the journey that God was taking us on together. Rachel's life was changed in every way, just as mine was. God had changed us both; now we were able to encourage one another and grow in faith together.

I knew I had to do certain things to help my faith to grow and develop, so I began reading the Bible every day. We went to church at the weekend and, during the week, attended Bible studies. I studied relentlessly. I was like a sponge, absorbing everything. I was captivated by what I was reading.

I still struggled. One moment I would be revelling in God's peace and the next moment an "old" thought would hit me like a right hook: "It won't last ... it never does, remember?" My heart would sink. I sensed I was in some kind of battle to hold onto this new life. Looking back, God was teaching me to live in the present moment and immerse myself in His presence. The more I was willing to submit to Him and receive His power, the more He was able to chip away my hard shell and renew me. It is one of the great paradoxes of the Christian faith, I have found, but in order to be strong, we have to become weak. The degree to which we surrender to God and give Him control is the degree to which He is able to strengthen us. I used to think that clenching my fist and hitting out made me strong and that surrendering made me weak. But God wanted to give me an inner strength that meant I didn't need to ball my hand into a fist. Instead I needed to open my hands to Him and say, "Lord, help me in my weakness; give me your strength."

A friend of mine would always say, "Live for now." For many that is a just a figure of speech. We can all agree that the only thing that exists at this moment is what's happening right now. Right now you are reading this book. In a few moments you'll be in another moment, perhaps putting the book down and making a cup of tea. "Now" will never happen again. Eventually, I realised that I couldn't turn my mind on and off, but I could renew my mind to work differently; to think and believe God's words. I told myself that if I didn't take control of my mind then my mind would take control of me. I knew I had to start forgetting those former problems and not dwell on my past all the time.

Many years ago farmers would have had to plough their fields by hand, since there was no machinery in those days. To keep the furrows straight the farmer would have to keep his eyes fixed on a tree in the distance ahead of him, or place a stake in the ground. If he turned around to look back at the field he was ploughing before he'd reached his final destination, he'd put a kink in his furrow, resulting in the rest of the field being off balance.

This was like me. I had been trying to live in the present moment, but I kept looking back at my old beliefs and running off course. If I did this constantly, then maybe my life would eventually go in completely the wrong direction again. I needed to focus on Jesus and not look back. I didn't want anything to distract me from following Him, especially not my past. Of course, we can reminisce about good times; get the photos out and look back over them. But going over past hurts and pain, dwelling on the time we spent in prison – that will rob us of the joy of the present.

There is a very real spiritual dimension to life on earth and I believe that we are engaged in a very real, spiritual battle against forces of darkness that would like to see our lives destroyed. I know this sounds dramatic, but I believe it with all my heart. Forces intent on our destruction want us to focus on the wrong things and keep us living in the past, instead of moving forward into our future. There are certain, negative emotions that, if we give them free reign will put us straight back in prison. In the next section of this book I want to identify what these are and give you some important keys to living and staying free.

10

EMOTIONS THAT KEEP US IMPRISONED

Whenever a person suffers a trauma in their life, emotional scarring results. The worse the trauma, the worse the emotional wreckage that follows. Sometimes people think that they are unaffected by the bad things that have happened in their past, but there is always a price to pay. People will often find themselves being ambushed by their emotions later on, when they least expect it, and then find themselves spiralling out of control.

I found that I suffered a variety of uncontrolled emotions after all of my mental and physical torture. The most prevalent was sheer anger, but a number of other emotions came with it. Such emotions distort our view of ourselves and, as a result, lead us to believe lies about ourselves.

For example, we feel shame and this seeds the thought that we are worthless. This lie then becomes destructive in our life, causing us to behave in counterproductive ways, exposing ourselves to more shame, which then leads to more emotional fallout and further lies. It is a terrible, vicious cycle. The only way to break out of this downward spiral is by feeding on God's truth – the truth of who we are in Jesus. Here are some of the things that I was battling with, which I'm sure are common to so many.

The first was irrational fear. It began as real fear, of course, because I lived daily with the very real threat of being pursued and beaten by bullies. I was frightened to go to school; frightened of being tied up and battered. I was frightened of being sexually abused, yet too scared to break free from the control my abuser held over me. Later, however, this real fear turned into irrational fear: the fear of entering an empty house on my own; the fear that any of this might happen to me again or that I might allow anyone to have control over me again. This caused me to violently attack others. I wanted to hit them before they hit me; I wanted to be the one who was in control, causing fear in others. Fear also manifest itself in a constant paranoia. I couldn't escape the thought that at any moment, everything was going to go wrong. Fear is like a self-fulfilling prophecy: if we expect something to go wrong, it probably will. Our behaviour can dictate that. We may have real fears in our life, based on actual situations, but mostly our fears are unfounded. We spend vast amounts of time worrying about things that haven't happened yet and may never happen.

Shame was a paralysing emotion for me. I walked around feeling disgraced and disgusting, especially because of the sexual abuse. I felt humiliated and this reduced my self-worth to sub-zero levels. Shame is a disturbing thing when you consider that it can lower a person's self-esteem to the point where they become vulnerable to further abuse. A person with no self-worth expects others to use and abuse them.

Closely linked to shame is guilt. It is a common phenomenon that people who have been abused feel a huge amount of guilt, thinking that in some way, what happened was their fault. They feel that they must have done something to cause the awful things happening to them and feel they are somehow to blame. I had my fair share of guilt, not just because of what I suffered, but also because of the pain I inflicted on so many others. I felt guilty for causing my mam and dad so much anxiety and pain. I felt guilty about all the people I'd physically hurt. I felt guilty about leaving my kids. All of this added to my misery and feelings of worthlessness. Guilt is a heavy burden to carry.

Then there was jealousy. All my suffering left me feeling incredibly insecure and plagued by negative thoughts. I was insecure and jealous in any relationship and would constantly turn in on myself, drowning in thoughts of inadequacy, uncertainty, resentment, even disgust with myself. I felt weak and unloved.

But by far the biggest emotion that dogged me was anger. Anger gripped me and frequently took over, sending me out of control. I was angry with myself that somehow I had allowed all these bad things to happen to me; angry that I had allowed myself to be controlled; angry that people had taken advantage of me; angry with anyone who dared to try and cross me again.

Sometimes I was utterly consumed by thoughts of revenge for all that had happened. This caused me many problems. It derailed my relationships, frequently got me into trouble with the police, caused trouble at work and caused violence to erupt at the slightest provocation. The consequences of my anger were always dire. I would swear, shout, push people around and then lash out. I was a walking time bomb. But in my anger I also plotted a terrible revenge on those who had bullied and abused me. Thankfully, God saved me from acting out that revenge.

I would also turn my anger inwards, on myself. Because I knew I could be so violent, I would bottle the anger up and try to contain it. Then I became like a pressure cooker, simmering and boiling. I had a debilitating self-hatred. Eventually this led to depression.

I didn't know how to deal with any of these negative emotions. I was just trapped. But when God came into my life, He began to show me how I could reverse the destructive processes that operated in my life.

It sounds a very simple thing to say – because it is simple, yet at the same time, deeply profound – but the only antidote to lies is the truth – God's truth. I've said a couple of times in this book that it seemed as though my life was playing out to a negative inner script. My traumatic experiences had programmed into me a set of dangerous, damaging beliefs; beliefs that dictated my actions and ultimately caused those beliefs to become even more deeply embedded. God showed me that I needed reprogramming. I needed to have all those lies overwritten, erased by the truth.

Let me explain a bit more. When a person gives their life to Christ, they are made new. The Bible refers to them as a "new creation" and states that the old has gone and the new has come (2 Corinthians 5:17). This re-creation triggers the start of an on-going transformation, as God makes us more and more like Jesus. When we become a Christian, our whole identity changes. We are now wanted and loved by a perfect Father; we are valued and cherished; we have a purpose and an exciting future mapped out for us. The list goes on and on.

We need to connect with the truth of who we are in Christ in order to break free from who we used to be before. As part of this process of change, our mind gets renewed over time. We are free to begin to think differently. Instead of negative, destructive patterns of thought dictating our behaviour, we can have life-giving, positive thoughts that set a new path. But this doesn't just happen automatically, we have a part to play: we have to immerse ourselves in the truth and we do that by reading the Bible, God's Word.

The Apostle Paul who wrote a big chunk of the New Testament had some advice for believers: "Don't copy the behaviour and customs of this world, but let God transform you into a new person by changing the way you think. Then you will learn to know God's will for you, which is good and pleasing and perfect" (Romans 12:2 NLT). The Message version of the Bible puts it even more simply than this: "Fix your attention on God. You'll be changed from the inside out."

What I had to do to find peace, healing and transformation was to focus on truths in the Bible relevant to my problems. As I dwelled on those truths, the tide of darkness was pushed back. Here are some of the scriptures that helped me stop the tide of negativity. These verses are about anger, but there are verses that cover every human problem!

"Stop being angry! Turn from your rage! Do not lose your temper—it only leads to harm ... the wicked will be destroyed, but those who trust in the Lord will possess the land." (Psalm 37:8 NLT)

"The Lord is gracious and compassionate, slow to anger and rich in love." (Psalm 145:8)

"A gentle answer deflects anger, but harsh words make

tempers flare." (Proverbs 15:1 NLT)

"[Love] does not dishonour others, it is not self-seeking, it is not easily angered, it keeps no record of wrongs." (1 Corinthians 13:5)

"Get rid of all bitterness, rage and anger, brawling and slander, along with every form of malice." (Ephesians 4:31)

Numerous times in the Bible we read the words "fear not", "do not fear" or "don't be afraid". We also read "don't worry" or "don't be anxious". Throughout the Bible there is a clear theme: the only thing we are to fear is God Himself (and in the Bible this doesn't mean to be afraid of God, but to have an "awe" and "respect" for Him). We are to trust God and not be afraid of anything. God is love and as John, the friend of Jesus, wrote: "There is no fear in love. But perfect love drives out fear..." (1 John 4:18).

God has also dealt with the issues of guilt and shame. Romans chapter 8 verse 1 says clearly: "There is no condemnation for those who belong to Christ Jesus" (NLT). And Paul wrote, "Anyone who believes in him will never be put to shame" (Romans 10:11).

When we come to God and surrender our lives, He welcomes us into His presence. In His presence we find that our fears are taken away. As we trust in Him, He cleanses our guilty conscience. Then He lifts up our head and restores our dignity, taking away all our shame. God took the shame I used as a tool of cruelty on myself and turned it into joy.

At this point you may be thinking, this all sounds too easy. Let me say this in response: it is far from easy, but it's not impossible. If God can take hold of my life, desperate as it was, and transform me into a completely different person, He can do the same for you. No one is beyond redemption. My journey has been long and hard. At times, issues in my life have looked like insurmountable mountains; too high to get over, too wide to get around, too deep-rooted to dig up. But God has shown me that if I trust in Him, He can literally crush those obstacles and make a way for me to walk, unhindered, from A to B. Regardless of the mountains you are facing in your life right now, God is so much bigger and more powerful. Nothing is impossible for Him. Trust God and He will walk you through the pain and the trials. Trust in Jesus and He will make His home in your heart, cause you to flourish, and keep you strong. If you let Him in, He will pour His incredible love into your heart.

In the Bible Jesus tells us not to worry about tomorrow, because tomorrow will worry about itself. Each day has enough trouble of its own (Matthew 6:34). Jesus reassures us that His presence is constantly with us and when we are aware of this truth, it fills us with peace. We may not always feel as though God is on our side, but as we've already learnt, feelings are poor indicators of the truth. Our feelings are fickle and misleading; the truth is always true – no matter what. I had to learn to live each day mindful of the fact that God was with me and loved me, no matter what. I refused to allow feelings of worry and doubt to fester, because Jesus had promised never to leave me and told me not to worry.

My prayer is that you can find and enjoy the depths of the peace of God too. Learning how to tame your negative thoughts is key to this. In the following chapter we will take a closer look at the battle that takes place in our mind.

11

WINNING THE BATTLE FOR OUR MIND

One of the biggest lessons I've learnt on my journey is that if we want to live free from the past, we need to change our thinking. I was continually beset by negative, self-destructive thoughts. I needed to fill my mind with positive, life-giving thoughts. Let me be clear: I'm not talking about some kind of "positive thinking" technique. There is no doubt that thinking/being positive has a good effect on a person's life, but it can't overcome the effects of deep, lasting, emotional scars. All it can ever do is paper over the cracks. In order for real inner transformation to take place, a person has to feed on a diet of God's life-changing truth.

When you become a Christian, the spiritual dimension of life opens up before you. I began to realise that I wasn't just engaged in an emotional battle, but a spiritual one – and the primary battlefield was my mind. I needed to embrace the truth of what God said about me and embed those beliefs inside me, so that they would ultimately lead to a change of behaviour.

As I did this, replacing my old beliefs and habits with new ones, anxiety and doubt began to melt away and fear was replaced with faith. I mentioned earlier that trust was a huge issue for me. I found it almost impossible to trust others. Ironically, the one thing I had to learn to do was to trust God! I had to trust Him to take care of everything in my past, trust Him for my present, and trust Him for everything in the future. I had massive control issues too – and God needed to be in control of my life before He could turn it around and make it a success. I guess I couldn't have trusted Him or allowed Him to take control of my life if He hadn't first shown me that He loved me – completely, fully, unreservedly – and had my best interests at heart. The key to letting go is realising that if we allow God to take control of our lives He will lead us into the best life possible.

Over time I've learnt not to keep delving into my past and rehearsing the pains and hurts that lie there. I'm still learning not to keep speculating about the future and worrying what might happen. There is a big difference between planning for our future and allowing ourselves to be filled with fear and anxiety about things that haven't even happened yet. Focusing too heavily either on the future or the past has the potential to drag us down. Instead we need to learn to live increasingly in the present moment, trusting God to work out everything. This is a discipline that can be developed.

Now, whenever I notice that my thoughts are running off into the past (or future), I remind myself that I need to feed my mind with something more helpful. Eventually, the thoughts we feed ourselves with are the thoughts that win.

One of my friends says, "We're always full of something." It may be anger, bitterness or criticism or it may be love, joy and peace. But whatever we are full of will eventually spill out of us.

I had feasted on a diet of negativity for years. I had said bad things about myself over and over again, like I had my finger stuck on the rewind button. Looking in the mirror, disgusted with myself, I would stick labels on myself like, "failure ... waste of space ... hopeless ...". Then I would speak out self-fulfilling prophecies, such as, "I'll never change ... things will never be any different ... nothing works out for me ... everything goes wrong ... I'll never be happy...".

I'd said these things so often that I had come to believe them. Even though they were lies, I was convinced they were true. I'd play that tape over and over, until I was sick to death of it. It caused nothing but pain. I was an emotional desert, my soul a parched wasteland. Every negative thought dehydrated my life a bit more and sucked more and more life out of me.

Nowadays, I spend some time alone with God every morning, reading His Word and drinking in its truth. It revives and refreshes me. The Bible says that, as a person thinks so they will be (Proverbs 23:7). If I begin to dwell on things that I don't want to become, it gives me an unpleasant feeling, as though I'm about to unlock a door I don't want to enter. I remember what it was like to be locked inside that prison with those destructive thoughts as my companions.

I don't want to go back there.

Instead, I stay close to God and renew my mind with His help.

If you don't believe that taming the mind is vital to being transformed, try this little experiment: try getting angry without first having angry thoughts. Or try feeling sad without first having sad thoughts or dwelling on some sad event, situation or personal loss. It can't be done. In order to experience a feeling, we first need to have the thought that stimulates it. This is why we need to win the battle for our mind.

A change of identity: from weakness to strength

I've already mentioned that when we become a Christian we receive a new identity. It takes a while to "grow into" this new identity as we discover all the things that have become true about us. But just because this process takes time, it doesn't mean those things are not real or true now.

I like the character of Gideon in the Bible (see the book of Judges, chapters 6 and 7). God called him "a mighty man of fearless courage". This was his identity as far as God was concerned, but Gideon felt weak; he didn't see it. When God spoke this over him, Gideon's first reaction was: "He can't be talking about me. I come from the poorest family and I am the least one in my father's house." Gideon saw himself as weak and defeated. He had locked himself in the same prison cell that I occupied for so many years. God saw the treasure in Gideon, however – strong, confident, a leader, a warrior. Gideon's dilemma was: should I believe what God says about me or believe my own thoughts and feelings? This is the choice we all have to make.

I felt weak, but I came to realise that God wanted to make me strong. I had been afraid for years, but God wanted to make me confident. I thought it was impossible for me to forgive, but He said, "All things are possible with me" (Matthew 19:26). God touched my life. He took off all of those labels I had pinned on myself. He cancelled all the self-fulfilling, negative predictions I made about my life. He mapped out a new future for me. Now I had to make a conscious choice to agree with what God said about me, rather than what I said about myself.

I recall one time when Rachel and I visited an 88-year old lady in hospital who was about to have a small operation. As we chatted to her, she began to reminisce about her life. She quickly brought up an incident that had happened to her when she was 15. She recalled how it had affected her and how sad it made her feel, to the point where she burst into tears in front of us. 73 years later she was still feeling the pain of this event. In order to experience such strong emotions she must have rehearsed that event over and over in her mind.

The power of our thoughts is incredible. They define our identity. That's why the Bible says, "Guard your heart above all else, for it determines the course of your life" (Proverbs 4:23). Like millions of other people, my heart had been wounded. It became a very poor navigation system for my life. Thankfully, God mended my heart and, with His truth at its centre, I was on the right track.

I am still amazed at how much life has changed for me. I am only too aware that my life now sounds so completely different than in the first half of this book. This is the power of God to change a person. My life was like an untended garden, slowly suffocating under an impenetrable tangle of weeds. Now my garden is being renovated by the Master Gardener. The weeds are being pulled out, the grass cut, the borders raked and cultivated, the ground seeded and fed. What was slowly atrophying has been brought back to life.

It's interesting in the Bible that when Jesus was tempted by the devil in the wilderness, the enemy immediately questioned His identity. He knew that if he could undermine Jesus' beliefs about who He was and what He was called to do, he could make Him fall. Jesus defended Himself by speaking out the truth, quoting passages of Scripture (read the beginning of Matthew 4 for the full story). At other times when Jesus faced temptations or trials, it was His knowledge of Scripture that protected Him. This is why it is so important to rely on the truth of what God says about us, rather than our feelings. Renewing our mind can feel like hard work at times, but just as a house is built one brick at a time, so our lives are changed one thought at a time. The only way we're going to be truly changed, permanently transformed, is by renewing our minds with the Word of God.

Living it out...

A friend of mine, Ken, who has helped me with my Bible studies, often says, "God's Word has to be lived out; its not just knowledge for the mind." Every day I am learning to act upon the truth I read. If we are just reading nice words, closing our Bibles and saying, "That's nice", then living no differently – what use is that? We need to live out what we read, otherwise they are just words.

There's a story in the Bible where Jesus delivers a child from a bad spirit. The child's father asks, "Can you do anything to help him?" Jesus's response is, "Everything is possible for him who believes." Immediately the boy's father cries out, "I do believe; help me overcome my unbelief!" (Mark 9:24).

Anything I tried to do in my life whilst I was still holding on to other beliefs was an absolute failure. When I started to rid myself of those beliefs by thinking and then acting differently, I saw my life begin to change in every area. My beliefs were motivating my actions and my actions were producing the results in my life. If you look at your life and you don't like the results you're getting at the moment, you need to change your beliefs, which in turn will change your actions. You have to choose to fill your life with truths that will lead to an inner transformation and a positive outcome. As the saying goes, "If you always do what you've always done, you'll always get what you've always got."

Many of us are like the father who pleaded with Jesus, "Help me overcome my unbelief." But if we put our trust in God, ask Him to help us, and believe Him for the outcome, He will never let us down. He has the keys to any and every prison we may find ourselves in.

Once I didn't even believe that there was a God. Now I do believe and I have no more sleepless nights; no more hatred boiling up in me. I am no longer haunted by my past. I believe what God has to say about me and live in the present moment. I don't want to sound arrogant by saying this, like I suddenly know it all. I don't. But I found freedom and I am passionate about helping others to get free too. As someone once said, "I'm just one beggar telling another beggar where he found bread."

12
THE KEY OF FORGIVENESS

For many years I relied on my fists for my strength. Attack was my method of self-defence. I wanted to hurt before anyone could hurt me. I wanted to take control in order to feel in control; to control others before they controlled me. Little did I realise that forgiveness was going to become my greatest strength and my best defence.

Forgiveness is a difficult subject for someone who has been hurt and abused. When others abuse us the desire for payback is deep. Bitterness and resentment easily take hold and fuel feelings of anger and revenge. I was full of negative thoughts towards my abusers. Forgiving those who had hurt me, in mind or body, was a grim prospect. But forgiveness had to be part of the process of letting go of the past. It was the hardest thing I've ever done.

When I began to find myself living more in the present and less in the past or future, God was finally able to help me deal with the issue of forgiveness. I felt Him saying to me, "You need to forgive your abuser and everyone else who's hurt you." My first reaction to this was: "There's not the remotest possibility that I will ever forgive the people who hurt me so severely!" In my mind, forgiving those who had deliberately chosen to beat me and sexually abuse me when I was a kid would make me weaker than I was then. It would be like giving into them all over again. They would be gaining the victory once more.

Once we've been hurt, our natural tendency is to build a wall, make a defence, stop it happening again. We do it to keep out those who may potentially harm us. But this is counterproductive for two reasons: first, it keeps everyone out, not just those who might hurt us, and so we become cold and distant. Second, it keeps us in – we are locking ourselves inside an emotional prison. This is an unhappy, lonely place to be. We begin to wallow in self pity. "How can God love me?" we say and our pain answers the question: "That's right. No one loves you." Can I urge you not to go down that well-trodden path again? I've been there many times myself; it doesn't lead anywhere good.

The breakthrough came for me when God showed me that it wasn't my abusers who needed this act of forgiveness, it was me. Someone has said, "Harbouring unforgiveness is like drinking poison and hoping the other person will die." Unforgiveness is indeed a poison to the soul. It infects us with bitterness, anger, depression, resentment, hopelessness and more. I needed to forgive because unforgiveness was like an anchor to my past. All the while I held onto it, I would never be free. Not forgiving people who have abused you in the past, means that you are continuing to give them power over your present.

Because I was holding on to my anger and hatred, in effect, I was still being abused. This brought me more weakness and more pain. No matter how much I thought they needed to be punished for what they'd done, holding onto it would only perpetuate the sadness, hurt, anger and everything else.

As RT Kendall has pointed out, often people are reluctant to forgive because it feels as though we are either condoning what they did or simply letting them off. God showed me that they weren't being let off, since He holds every person accountable for their life and actions, and neither was I condoning what they'd done. This was about freeing me from my past.

Blaming others for our unhappiness saps our energy. If you are reading this book and thinking, "I can't forgive..." I have to tell you that you can. Don't doubt yourself; you're better than that. You can go beyond this because you have a choice. I had a choice: either I could carry on living in my pain and suffering or I could forgive and move forward with my life. I could move into the wholeness that Jesus wanted for me. By choosing to forgive I became a stronger person, not a weaker one.

The Bible commands us to, "Forgive whatever grievance you may have against one another. Forgive as the Lord forgave you" (Colossians 3:13). This is extremely challenging, but we have to choose to forgive others out of obedience to God, who knows how we are made and how we were designed to work. Humans were not designed to bottle up unforgiveness.

I can testify to the truth of this because unforgiveness had a very serious impact on my health. It robbed me of any sense of wellbeing and affected me physically. It has been medically proven that holding on to the feelings of bitterness and anger that unforgiveness produces can lead to depression, stress, stomach ulcers, high blood pressure, mood swings, migraines and even heart attacks. The strategy of bottling everything up wasn't working for me and it won't work for you. I chose to forgive for the sake of my long term health and wellbeing. I urge you to do the same.

Forgiveness is a process. It doesn't just happen overnight; it's a journey. I had many questions for God on my journey. I had very strong feelings about my abusers being punished for what they'd done. I often asked God why I had to forgive those who'd hurt me so much. He told me to accept His help and healing and to trust Him with all my heart. He said that if I continued to bury my hurt, it would end up robbing me of the life He had given me. He also showed me that just as anger masks unforgiveness towards others, shame and guilt mask unforgiveness towards ourselves. I was surprised to learn that I needed to forgive myself, just as I needed to forgive my abusers. Both these aspects were blocking me from receiving God's peace and joy.

The test of forgiveness

Before God came into my life I was full of thoughts of revenge. I plotted the demise of my tormentors many times. But my resolve to forgive was put to the test when one particular man attacked and seriously hurt a member of my family. I was incensed. I couldn't contain the anger. I planned to hurt this person for what he'd done. It was going to be serious. I had specific plans – ones that could see me going to prison. In fact, I had factored this possibility into my thinking – planned for it, in case I was caught. In my heart I had decided that he had done something unforgiveable, and he had to pay.

So blinded was I by hatred that I never stopped to think what effect my actions would have on my wife and kids, my home or my business. Many times I drove by his home slowly, hoping that I'd see him, that the circumstances would be right and the opportunity to strike would present itself. This went on for several years. I tortured myself with thoughts of what I was going to do to him when I got hold of him. I began falling out with people I met who knew him. This man became a burden in my life. I was carrying him around with me everywhere when I should have forgiven him and let him go. Fortunately, I somehow never bumped into him to give him the payback I felt he deserved.

As I was walking through my healing process, God knew what was going on in my mind. He could see the constant battle I was fighting and how this man was never far from my thoughts. He helped me to see that even though this person was walking about in the area where I lived, I had to let him go, once and for all. I had to forgive him, not put him in hospital or worse. So I made a choice. I chose to forgive him and I meant it.

To prove that God knows me better than I know myself, a matter of hours after making this decision, I saw him on the street for the first time in years. For the previous five years I had been on the lookout for him and never saw him. Now he was walking down the street towards me. He knew who I was and I knew him. Our eyes met and he was startled. He stopped in his tracks, literally frozen with fear. He looked like a rabbit in the headlights, waiting for death. I looked him in the eyes but walked straight past him, as though I'd never seen him before in my life. The sense of the burden being lifted from my shoulders was immense. It was an indescribably great feeling to let go of that heavy baggage I'd been carrying around with me for so long. Some people might call me weak for doing this. I wasn't. It was one of the hardest things I've ever done.

As Martin Luther King Jr once said: "Darkness cannot drive

out darkness; only light can do that. Hate cannot drive out hate; only love can do that."

13

FORGIVENESS IN ACTION

I get to meet a lot of people in the course of running my tattoo studio and they often talk about the problems they are facing in life. It's amazing how often the issue of forgiveness comes up. Something I hear a lot is, "Okay, I might forgive them, but I'll never forget" or "I'll never be able to completely forgive them." When I hear these words, I understand. I used to say the same thing. Their thought patterns are the same as mine were: If I forgive them completely, they will have won and I'll be even weaker. This is a lie that keeps people in bondage to their past.

Many situations and people in our life can hurt us: our parents, siblings, friends, school teachers, husband or wife... but forgiveness is our greatest defence against hurt and its effects. I write this because I care. I care because I know what it's like to be locked up in sadness and pain for years on end. More importantly, I write because God cares about you and wants to set you free. Let me tell you about some of the people who've come through my studio...

One day, a troubled looking young guy came in to see me with a design of a cross. It looked really nice and we chatted about it, I quoted him a price and he was happy to go ahead. Then he asked if I would add some words underneath the cross: God forgives, but I don't. I immediately told him about my faith and said that I was very careful about what I tattooed on people. I didn't feel I could do this tattoo, but since he was obviously hurting about something, I asked him to tell me what was bothering him. After a few minutes of small talk he began to open up and tell me how he'd fallen out with his wife and hated her for preventing him from seeing his son.

I told him I understood completely how he must be feeling, but explained that hating his wife wouldn't do him any good. In fact, it would become toxic and damaging to him. I told him about the need for forgiveness and how it can set us free. He told me he understood what I was saying, thanked me and left the shop. Two weeks later he came back to see me. He had a big smile on his face. He told me he wanted the same tattoo of a cross, but asked if I would put his son's name underneath it. I agreed.

While I was doing the tattoo he told me he'd had a long think about the things I'd said. He'd decided that he wasn't willing to let his negative thoughts, anger and bitterness ruin the two things he loved most: his wife and his son. He had gone to visit his wife, this time like a completely different person. As a result they had resolved their differences and become a family once again.

On another occasion I was tattooing a man while his wife was sitting on the couch next to us. We were all chatting away when the conversation turned to our dads. I mentioned that mine had passed away. The lady immediately commented, punctuated with swear words, that her dad was "dead" too. I was struck by the anger in her voice as she said it.

God has the ability to speak into our minds and, as Christians, we can hear His voice as He guides and directs us or speaks to us about situations in our life. He can also speak "words of knowledge" through us. In other words, He can give us snippets of information about other people/situations that only He could possibly know. This is His way of getting a person's attention and saying, "I know all about what you're going through and I care about you."

I felt God speak to me about this lady, so I replied, "Obviously your dad isn't dead, I can hear it in your voice. He must have hurt you very badly."

This took her by surprise, but then she began ranting about her dad. "Hurt me? I've not spoken to him since I was 18. I've been married nearly 15 years; I've got a son who's 10 and a daughter who's 7. He's never seen either of them and I bet he doesn't even care. And not once has he ever told me that he loves me either."

I felt God say to me that this was because her dad had been abused as a child. "Have you ever asked your dad why?" I asked her.

She gave a hollow laugh, trying to disguise the pain in her eyes. "No, I haven't. Anyway, how can I? I told you, in my eyes he's dead."

I told her I was a Christian.

"Oh, here we go!" she exclaimed. "I don't want to talk about all that rubbish."

I smiled at her. "You may think it's rubbish, but God has just shown me why your dad is the way he is. I don't believe it's for me to tell you though. If you know or can find out where your dad's living, ring him up. God is telling me that your dad will tell you the truth."

She wasn't having any of this. "Thanks, but no thanks," she said, in effect, punctuated with a stream of obscenities. I finished her husband's tattoo and the couple left. I could tell from the look on her face as she exited the studio that she wasn't rushing home to add me to her Christmas card list.

About ten months later, however, the same couple turned up at my shop. This woman walked in, her face radiant, and greeted me warmly. "Hello Swanny, how are you my friend?" she began. I didn't recognise her; she was like a different person. "You don't remember me, do you?" she guessed correctly. "Sorry, no!" I admitted. She then proceeded to remind me of her story.

"I'm the lady who said my dad was dead, remember? Let me tell you what happened. After we left your shop, I was so angry with you for what you'd said that I called you names all the way home. In fact, all that night I was saying to my husband, 'Who does he think he is, telling me to ring my dad? He doesn't even know my dad. Telling me that God had told him all about it… don't make me laugh!'"

"Well, I went to bed that night and I couldn't get your words out of my mind and couldn't sleep. The same happened the next night and then the next. Three nights in a row I couldn't get your words out of my head, so I decided to contact my dad. I found it very hard to do. Like I told you, the last time we spoke was when I was 18. My dad asked if we could meet. He didn't really want to talk on the phone, but said that for many years he'd been longing for this day."

"So we met. I told him that I'd been speaking to this Christian bloke who said if I called, my dad would explain why he'd never ever said he loved me. Dad then sat me down and told me that when he was a little boy he'd been sexually abused. When I was born, he was so excited and proud, but also so full of fear. He was afraid of getting too close to me, worried that he might start doing the same things to me that someone had done to him – and that was too much for him to handle. All he wanted to do was love me, but because of this burden he had to lose his only daughter instead."

By now, the tears were running down her face. Then she said, "And do you know what, Swanny? We had a hug and we never leave each other now without having one. I forgave him and the forgiveness has healed everything. I've learnt to let go of my grudge. We're all so happy. Thank you for taking the risk to say what you said."

I told her, "This is a lovely story. I'm so happy for all of you. But it's not me you should be thanking, it's God. He's the one who told me."

"I know," she said with great meaning. "I believe that. So does my dad. We'll never stop thanking Him."

Forgiveness is a powerful thing. It had restored the relationship of a dad and his daughter that looked lost forever. Grudges can so easily turn into hatred. It's important to deal swiftly with them. It took me a long time to forgive others and I nursed those grudges for far too long. It caused me a great deal of pain and sapped the life out of me. In time, the act of forgiveness helped turn my life around.

Without forgiveness we harbour resentment and bitterness and it eats away at our soul like a disease. If we're not careful, the weight of bitterness and resentment will pull us down into depression and anxiety. We store up the other person's wrongs, committed against us, and think about how we'd like to give them the same treatment they gave us. The Bible encourages to be better than this, to take a different path:

"You should also be kind and humble. Don't be hateful and insult people just because they are hateful and insult you. Instead, treat everyone with kindness. You are God's chosen ones, and he will bless you." (1 Peter 3:8-9 CEV)

The stories above illustrate that, though we may have been the injured party, we can still take the initiative to forgive. With God's help, we can set in motion the healing process. We're not dependent on those who have hurt us making the first move. Jesus teaches us to not waste a minute: to make the first move, put things right, to do it now.

I underestimated the power of forgiveness, but I learnt that it's the one power I've always had, and still have, over those who hurt me. Forgiveness brought healing after years of abuse. It shows how God can bring good out of the darkest of situations.

I also had to work through the process of asking God to forgive all the wrong things I had done to others. I had hurt a great many people over the years because I was an angry man, furious with everything and everybody. I was blind with rage until God opened my eyes with His grace. If we're honest with ourselves, every one of us needs forgiveness. We've all done and still do wrong things and live in constant need of His grace. But God's grace is sufficient to cover all our failings and more.

I'm still far from perfect. I let anger beat me sometimes. I can still feel jealous, still judge others on occasion. When this happens I have to say sorry to God and accept His forgiveness once again. Living in His grace and forgiveness is a journey. Never say to yourself, "I'm hopeless … I can't forgive … I can't be forgiven." You're not hopeless and you can. Instead of looking inside, turn your focus towards God. He can help you. He will take away your pain. He did it for me and He will do it for you. Forgive and see what happens.

14
LOOKING UP

Before God took hold of my life and began to turn it around, I lived with a permanent feeling of hollowness. I was in an emotional vacuum; emotionally bankrupt. Though I had much to be thankful for – Rachel, the kids, a new career – I constantly fought off depression over my past, waking each day feeling more tired than the previous one. I remember thinking on numerous occasions, "I wish this heaviness would leave. I wish, I wish…"

I remember one day going for a walk to try to clear my head. It was dusk, the streets of Shelthorpe bathed in early Spring light. The weather was warm, but I felt a coldness inside. If you'd seen me that evening, you would have noticed me walking with slumped shoulders, weighed down with cares; head hanging, staring at the ground.

To me, life looked bleak, no matter what. Instead of recalling happy memories of lazy summers spent idling the time away, in my head I was on the run from the bullies again; pursued by the memory, if not the reality of them. Tears ran down my cheeks.

I was always looking down, staring at the floor. It was a physical expression of an inner reality: I had no self-confidence. The only time I looked anyone in the eye was when I was burning with anger, ready to hit out. The rest of the time I was beset by a huge amount of shame. I never looked up; never looked beyond my personal problems. As a result I shut out a great many people and many things in life I could and should have been grateful for.

I felt that the whole world was against me. A turning point came in my life when I understood for the first time that God was for me, not against me (Romans 8:31). For the first time, someone was on my side; totally for me, committed to helping me succeed in life. It blew my mind. There is an amazing verse in Psalm 3, which says,

"You, LORD, are a shield around me, my glory, the One who lifts my head high." (Psalm 3:3)

I gradually began to understand that God, in His grace, didn't judge me for my past – Jesus had already taken care of that. Instead, He accepted me and wanted to lift up my head. He wanted to get rid of all the shame and guilt of the past and help me walk, head held high, into His purpose for my life.

The realisation of this truth gave me two precious things: peace and hope. Peace to live in the present moment and rest, trusting God for everything. And hope, to entrust the future to Him, knowing He is in control, and not bury myself in anxiety over things that haven't happened yet.

I don't know where you are at this precise moment in your life – maybe you're immobilised by confusion, riddled with fear, or weighed down with depression. I do know that whatever state of mind you are in, God can lead you to a place of peace, hope and freedom. This is His will for every person. We just need to listen to His words and understand the truth.

Knowing God's truth about me finally made me look up. The grey clouds separated and I could begin to see blue sky. It changed my perspective on life – spiritually and naturally. Before I was barely aware of nature – birds, trees, flowers, natural beauty. Now I am constantly struck by the wonder of creation. Spiritually, my eyes were opened to see God's grace in action in the lives of those around me and that helped me see things differently too.

Spiritually speaking, I was a man dying of thirst and on the brink of starvation, when God pulled me back from the point of death. He showed me how to get food and water. Naturally speaking, when we're thirsty or hungry we just drink or eat. Normally, people don't deprive themselves of the basic sustenance for life to continue. But it's not uncommon for people to starve themselves of spiritual food and water. Naturally, we don't say to ourselves, "I ate and drank yesterday, so I don't need to do it today"; we understand that taking food and water is necessary each day for life to continue. But I've had to learn that in order to keep my soul healthy, I need to keep feeding on the truth; every day, a healthy diet – no spiritual hunger strikes. Now I spend time each day with God, feeding on the truth in the Bible and allowing His words to refresh my spirit.

Helen Keller wrote, "When one door of happiness closes, another opens, but often we look so long at the closed door we don't see the one which God has opened for us." I was an expert at staring at closed doors, seeing the negative, lacking any hope. I didn't even consider the possibility of the door to a brighter future opening for me until God helped me to see properly.

Happiness was an intangible concept to me; something elusive and far off. I rarely, if ever, smiled. But with God in my life I often caught myself smiling, even laughing – something previously unimaginable. Now I laugh easily – mostly at myself, but I laugh.

The Bible says, "A cheerful heart is good medicine, but a crushed spirit dries up the bones" (Proverbs 17:22). Jesus also said, "Do not let your hearts be troubled. Trust in God and trust also in me..." (John 14:1). Reading my story, you know that the only things I trusted in were my fists. I relied on my own strength. But it got me nowhere. I had to learn to trust in God's strength. Elsewhere in the Bible it says that His strength is made perfect in our weakness. In other words, where we are weak, God is strong. But even in those areas of life where we feel confident, God is stronger! We have to learn that we will only find peace and wholeness in full surrender to Him. That is the whole point of faith – to entrust our life to Him.

Learning patience

Paul, the pastor of my church, often reminds me to rely on God, not on myself. This is sound wisdom. But for someone with my background, who likes to take the initiative and make things happen, it's not always easy to achieve.

I remember one family holiday to Disney World in Florida when we visited a big water park. One of the attractions was called Lazy River. Basically, you sat in massive rubber rings that floated along with the flow of the water. The rings even had drinks holders and you could just sit there and chill out whilst being carried along. For a bit of fun my kids decided they would jump out of their rings and try swimming upstream for a bit. Because they were working against an undercurrent, however, they soon became exhausted. It was too much effort to go against the flow. Eventually they scrambled back into their rings and let the river take them on their journey.

It reminded me of my life: always struggling against the flow, swimming against the current. It didn't matter how strong I was or how hard I kicked against it, the tide always won. Just when I thought I was making progress, I was swept back to square one, cast adrift. God was teaching me that I needed to quit all that self-effort and allow Him to direct me. I had to flow in His direction and let Him carry me. My life didn't have to be a struggle for survival. Instead, I could embrace what The Message Bible calls the "unforced rhythms of God's grace".

I used to live in constant denial, trying hard to suppress my anger and fear. Through Christ I was learning to be more honest – with myself and others. Allowing myself to be still in God's presence slowed my heart rate and lowered my blood pressure; it was an antidote to the looming stress that always accompanied thoughts of my past. And yet, I was still in a rush. I knew God was taking me on a journey towards wholeness, but I wanted it now! I had to learn to be patient.

If God planted the seed of something good in my life, I wanted to see an oak tree the next day. That doesn't happen, not naturally, not spiritually. A seed that is planted needs to be watered and fed. Then it needs time to grow. A lot of the action happens under the surface, before the results are ever visible on the outside. When the green shoots finally break through the ground, it seems as though they've appeared overnight. But really, it's just another phase in a process that began long ago. I now believe that if God gave me whatever I asked for whenever I wanted it, I'd stop relying on Him and think it was all my own doing. God needs time to be able to grow and shape our character. When we are impatient and try to short cut His growth programme, we actually slow down the process and work against ourselves. In the end, the power of patience pays off.

Running along the back of our garden is a lane and in the hedgerow are dozens of blackberry bushes. Each year they produce their fruit and the kids from our estate come to pick them. On many occasions they come far too early and I tell them that the blackberries are not ripe enough to eat. If they'll wait just a few more weeks then they'll be sweet and tasty. Some of the kids don't take any notice and continue to pick them, but due to their sour taste most end up on the floor after they've spat them out. I felt God telling me that sometimes we are all like this. If we'd let God grow the blackberries they'd be a joy to eat, in His natural timing. But our lack of patience demands we eat from the bush when the fruit isn't fully ripe and then we complain that it tastes sour. How can God answer our impatient prayers on our terms? We have to trust that His timing is perfect.

Learning to love ourselves

One thing I always struggled with was simply being at peace with myself; loving myself, accept myself as I was. I realise now that this was a product of the guilt, anger and shame I felt. I've also learnt this is all too common. So many people have no self-confidence because of the experiences they've lived through. They often use degrading language when talking about themselves. God showed me that when we use this language He never agrees with us. He doesn't see us as fat, skinny, ugly, stupid, hopeless or whatever else we may say about ourselves.

He calls us precious, valuable and highly esteemed, so when we say those negative things we are actually in denial of the image He created.

People who don't love themselves are difficult to live with. I know, I was unbearable at times. How do we learn to love ourselves? The answer is trust. When we put our trust in God, self-confidence begins to rise up in us; we begin to discover our true identity as valued people. Remember the story of David in the Bible, who fought Goliath? Though David may have looked like a weak, skinny boy, he didn't act like one. He was full of confidence because he had full confidence in his God. He knew God was with him and for him.

Nowadays, instead of criticising myself constantly, I've learnt to love myself more. If I remember to be like David, to trust God and talk to Him about my problems, I know He'll give me the confidence I need. I have faith because I know that God is with me and will always be with me.

Jesus comes to anyone with a heart humble enough to accept Him. Whoever you are and whatever you've done, He'll come to you. The Bible says, "Do not worry about anything, instead; pray about everything. Tell God what you need and, thank Him for all He has done" (Philippians 4:6). If you take this advice, you will experience God's peace in your life – and His peace is a wonderful thing to experience.

We can learn to love ourselves when we realise that God accepts us as we are. He is not put off when we mess up and doesn't change His mind about us when we fail Him. Peter in the Bible is an inspiration to me. He followed Jesus and kept following Him, even though he made a lot of mistakes. He never did become a perfect person, but Jesus isn't looking for perfection; He's looking for real people with a heart to follow Him.

I often used to wonder what Jesus saw in me. I wondered what it was about me that made Him want me to follow Him. I'd failed so many times in my life. Yet I knew that Jesus accepted Peter in spite of his failures. Peter went on to do great things for God. I don't class myself as another Peter, far from it, but I do believe we can all achieve great things through Christ if we allow Him to guide us.

Surrender to Him and above all, remember to look up.

15

REBUILDING THE BROKEN WALLS

One of my inspirations for writing this book is to encourage others. I've tried to share with you some truths I've discovered. I certainly don't want to preach at you; I don't want to tell you how to live your life, that's totally in your hands. But I do hope I can help you see things differently and, perhaps, help you find peace like I did.

There is a story in the Old Testament that has encouraged me greatly and I trust it will give you hope too. It's about rebuilding that which has been broken.

Nehemiah was a cupbearer to a Persian king. The cupbearer tasted the wine before the king drank it, to ensure it wasn't poisoned. It was a position of great trust. The story tells us that Nehemiah heard of a great sadness that was overshadowing his people, back in his home city of Jerusalem. They were distressed and ashamed because the wall surrounding the city had been broken down and the city gates were burned down. This was bad news. It made his homeland vulnerable, because the city wall provided protection and security. The strength of the wall symbolised a city's strength and peace. Nehemiah was so upset about this that he sat down and cried. He cried out to God to forgive his people of their sins – the things they'd done which had led to this current state of affairs. Then Nehemiah had an idea: he ought to do something about it himself. But how?

A few days later, Nehemiah was doing his job, but his sadness was evident to the King. It was obvious he was distressed. The King asked him why he looked so sad. Nehemiah was fearful to share his thoughts, wondering how the King might react, but he nevertheless began to explain about his people's dilemma. The King looked at Nehemiah and asked him what he could do to help. Before he answered, Nehemiah prayed to God, then he asked the King's permission to be allowed to go and rebuild the wall. He would need various letters of passage written to allow him to cross the borders of neighbouring countries on his journey and also soldiers to protect him. The King granted all his requests and sent him on his way with his blessing. Not everyone was pleased he was going off to help the Israelites, however.

The journey was long, but when Nehemiah finally arrived, he inspected the wall and told the people of Jerusalem what he was going to do. He explained that God had been kind enough to grant his prayers and that the King had given him permission to come. They all agreed they should help to rebuild the wall of the city and restore it to its full splendour, one stone at a time.

It wasn't as simple a task as it should have been. Nehemiah faced opposition. Some people just thought he was crazy and ridiculed him. Others, who had a vested interest in keeping Jerusalem vulnerable, were more militant than that and tried to use threats, intimidation and force. Nehemiah kept his resolve, however, and kept his faith in God. He encouraged those helping him to keep going and not be intimidated. Brick by brick the wall was rebuilt.

What I find interesting is that Nehemiah's focus was on the work of rebuilding. He didn't get distracted and stop to fight those who were trying to stop him – he just carried on regardless. He simply prayed and asked God to deal with the people who wanted him to fail and to shame them. Nehemiah said to those around him, "Don't be afraid ... remember the Lord, who is great and awesome ... our God will fight for us" (Nehemiah 4:14-20)

I love this story because it reminds me of how I was – like a ruined wall. With the help and care of a patient builder who wasn't willing to leave me in that broken down state, I was rebuilt, stone by stone, layer by layer.

I had thought of myself as strong, having built a protective wall around myself. But actually, my wall was in ruins and I couldn't see it. In fact, things were worse than I imagined, because my whole life was built on a faulty foundation. My entire life was set to fall like a house of cards at any moment. The bricks I'd used to build my life were defective and crumbled easily. The foundation I'd built my life on was no better than shifting sand. I had to go right back to the beginning and allow God to set me on the right foundation and then build me, brick by brick, using the right materials.

Jesus told a parable about a foolish man who built his house on sand and a wise man who built his house on a rock. When the storms of life hit, the house on the rock stood firm while the house on the sand was swept away. Elsewhere in the Bible Jesus is identified as being "the rock". In other words, if we build our lives on Him as the foundation, the storms of life won't overwhelm or destroy us. Without Him at the centre, however, we are liable to be swept away and lost.

God is a master builder. He knows how to build a life perfectly. He miraculously creates masterpieces out of wreckage. He will lay the correct foundation for your life, if you let Him, and then make you into something amazing. Stones of grace, love, mercy and freedom, laid one on top of the other, will build a life that will never be shaken.

The power of persistence

After Nehemiah had finished his rebuilding work, you'd think that was the end of the story. But his detractors still went on ridiculing and intimidating him. The same thing happens when we commit our lives to Christ. To some, being a Christian seems quaint and old fashioned. To others it seems foolish and misguided – no better than believing in Father Christmas or the Easter Bunny. Then there are those who view faith as a crutch they can do without, thinking that it's for the weak or simple minded. How wrong people can be! Being a real Christian is no walk in the park. It's a life filled with risk and adventure; a life that stretches us to the limit, but then offers unbelievable rewards. Faith is no soft option.

Being a Christian means being involved in a spiritual battle. Discovering that God was real lifted the lid for me on the spiritual dimension to life. I found that the devil was real and intent on destroying people's lives just as Jesus is focused on rebuilding them. The forces of darkness come against us with a campaign of lies and deceit, designed to keep us locked up and far from freedom. But Christ came to destroy the works of the enemy and lead us to freedom.

What this means for me is that the enemy will persist in trying to rob me of my freedom. He'd like nothing more than to put me back in my cell, the self-destructive cycle of my past – both to ensure my demise and stop me from spreading the news of God's freedom to others. It is a very real battle. Sometimes he'll use other people to mock me. Since I became a Christian I've had my fair share of people laughing at me, criticising me (calling me a hypocrite etc) and saying that I've gone mad. It's a sad fact, but sometimes when we begin to make progress in life, the jealous, the critical and the small-minded come out of the woodwork and try to drag us back down to their level. We mustn't allow this to pull us off course.

At other times the enemy will prod my emotions and try to tell me I'm too weak and useless to be of any good to God. This is one of his key strategies: to make us believe we have to impress God by being good; that we have to perform in order to "earn" His love and favour. This is a lie. God saves us by His grace and there is nothing we can do that will make Him love us any less or any more. God loves each of us perfectly.

Though He accepts you and me just as we are, it doesn't mean God is content to leave us that way. He wants to restore the building – recreate the life – and make us into who we were supposed to be. How we were destined to be before people, circumstances and life damaged us and made us dysfunctional. Once again, we need to trust God. He knows what's best for us.

Once again, I'm not perfect – far from it. But I will never stop aiming for the target: to allow God to make me into all He planned for me to be. I still get hurt, I still get sad, I still get angry, like anyone. But the Great Restorer has given me a new foundation to stand on; one that is rock solid. With Jesus, I have the foundation to weather the storms of life.

Restoring others

I once heard a story about a depressed woman who had made up her mind to commit suicide. She threw herself from a bridge, aiming to drown in the icy waters below. A man saw her and without thinking instinctively plunged in to try and save her. He wasn't a strong swimmer though and, unused to open water, was soon in worse difficulty himself. Hearing his cries, the woman had a change of heart. She hauled him out of the water and ended up giving him life-saving mouth-to-mouth resuscitation. She responded to a need greater than her own and it changed her. She returned to her own life with a different perspective.

We all need help. I was like that drowning man, submerged in murky waters, thrashing around trying to stay afloat. God hauled me out of danger and breathed new life into me. It changed my perspective. I began to see that others were in need. There were people drowning all around me and I had the ability to do something about it.

We reap what we sow in life. If you feel you are lacking love, go out of your way to show love to someone else. If you feel unhappy, go and show kindness and compassion to someone who needs it. See the best in others and you will be your best. Seek to understand and you will be understood. Listen and you will be heard. Give to others and you will receive. Jesus said, "Do to others as you would have them do to you" (Luke 6:31). This is God's golden rule for a rich life. Helping others is one amazing way in which God brings healing to us. Hundreds of years ago Teresa of Avila wrote, "Christ has no body but yours, no hands, no feet on earth but yours … yours are the hands with which He blesses all the world."

In time, as God worked in my life to rebuild it, I really began to grasp this principle. I volunteered at a local prison and helped prepare lads for their release back into society. There were so many troubled minds and broken hearts. I asked God to help me offer some support and encouragement. He helped me to help others find the path towards healing.

Some time later, Carole, a friend from church, asked me and another guy, Richard, if I'd like to help her run a soup kitchen in our town. Initially I said no, because I thought I was too busy. But God spoke to me about it and encouraged me to help run the soup kitchen instead of prison visiting.

The soup kitchen is based in Beacon Christian Centre, my home church, and now I'm glad that I agreed to get involved. We have a great team of volunteers and we are able to touch the lives of many people in our area. Some volunteers shop, some cook, some serve the food and drinks; others wash up, play board games with people off the streets or give Bible talks. Others assist those who need helping filling out forms. Many just sit and chat and listen to people tell their stories.

Here is a true story from America about the impact this simple ministry can have on people. A guy called Bill ended up living on the streets and became an alcoholic to numb the pain. One day someone told Bill about Jesus and he gave his life to God. God helped Bill dry out and start attending church. Things began to turn around for him. Then God put it on Bill's heart to begin helping at the soup kitchen. He showed great love and kindness to everyone who came in and soon became popular; everyone loved him. One night at the soup kitchen, someone asked if anyone would like to be prayed for. Another alcoholic stood up and said, "Yes, pray for me to be more like Bill." "Why do you want to be like Bill?" the speaker asked, surprised. "Wouldn't you like to be more like Jesus?" The man looked puzzled. "Why? Is Jesus like Bill?" he enquired. We are God's hands and feet to those in need.

The soup kitchen had only been open for a few weeks when a lad came in who was living on the streets. Alcohol had gotten the better of him. We didn't judge him; we just loved him and fed him. It wasn't long before he was asking questions and we were telling him about God's love. We explained in simple terms how the hurts of life can tie us up, but God is capable of untying every knot. He understood. A few weeks later he asked Jesus to come into his life and it was amazing to see the change that took place in him. A friend of ours, Dettie, jointly owns some properties that are used to help the homeless. In return for free accommodation, the people who stay there do some odd jobs and are helped to come off drink or drugs. They also begin studying to get some qualifications. Dettie took this lad in and helped him. Two years later he has a place of his own and God has restored his previously broken down relationship with his family. Now he is working with people who have drink and drug addictions themselves and is helping them to turn their lives around. It's wonderful to see how much he's grown – and all the glory must go to God.

We've seen many people come through the doors of the soup kitchen and end up giving their lives to Jesus. They get cleaned up and are helped with their problems. We've also seen many healings. A man named Mick came to see us one day. He was upset as he'd been having problems with his eyesight.

A consultant had told him he was gradually losing his eyesight and would probably be blind within the next few years. We told Mick that God still performs miracles today and that, if he wanted, we could pray for him. He said he wanted us to pray, so we did. Two weeks later he saw the consultant again for more tests. The consultant was puzzled and said that for some reason, Mick's eyes had "corrected themselves". We knew that God had restored His eyesight.

A whole family used to come regularly to the soup kitchen. The dad liked to chat to me privately, so we would find somewhere quiet to sit, chat and pray. One day he arrived in a terrible state. His son had been taken into care, his family were due to be evicted from their accommodation and he had a bad infection in his foot that the hospital was very concerned about. Added to this, he needed to go into rehab for treatment for his alcohol and drug problem, but the waiting list was many months long. He asked me to pray for him. I did, remembering that Jesus teaches we should believe God has already answered our prayers and thank Him for it. I did that. The man sat there and cried.

When I saw him again he told me that the next morning he'd gotten up, looked at his foot and it was completely healed. Once again, the doctors concluded that the body had somehow miraculously "healed itself". That same morning, a social services representative came to see him and explained that, after discussing things further, they'd had a change of heart and were going to send his son back home. Later, in the afternoon, they heard from the local council that they would be allowed to stay in their present accommodation and were going to receive some help. Amazingly, he then heard from his GP who told him, "It must be your lucky day, a place has become available and you can go into rehab in four day's time!" We were all so pleased and gave God all the praise and glory.

I hope these stories encourage you and give you faith. No matter how desperate your situation is, God wants to help you. He has said, "Come to me all you who are weary and carry heavy burdens and I will give you rest" (Matthew 11:28). God wants to relieve us of our burdens and then help others to find that same relief and hope. He is in the business of rebuilding lives.

PART THREE: WRITING A NEW FUTURE

16

SUPERNATURAL LIVING

Your past may have written a life story for you that is robbing you of any hope. God can rewrite that script and set you free from the past. More than that, He can write a new story for your future – one filled with peace, hope, purpose and fulfilment. God rewrote my story; He can rewrite yours too. In the next couple of chapters I will share some of the things God has done since I surrendered my life to Him. I pray these stories will encourage you on your own journey. I don't share them to make you think I am some kind of super-Christian. The point is, when we surrender ourselves to God, we become His vessel, a channel for Him to touch the lives of others. The more transparent we become, the more God can do miracles through us that touch the lives of others. It's all about Him; not about me.

* * *

One afternoon I visited one of Dettie's houses to see the lad I mentioned in the previous chapter. We were helping to get him back on track. As I was leaving the house, another lad walked into the living room and introduced himself. He too had gotten mixed up with drugs and found himself homeless. He'd become a Christian after speaking to Dettie and then moved in. As he was talking I heard God say to me, "He's struggling." I asked him if he was still using. "No," he said, "I'm clean."

"That's not what God is telling me," I responded kindly. The Lord had shown me that He was still using heroin. I told him that if he wanted God to heal him, he first of all had to be truthful with himself. He told me that he did believe in Jesus; that he'd had an amazing experience when he'd prayed and asked Him into his heart. But he found that the pain of his past was too much to bear; he needed the drugs to "take him away" from life sometimes. I told him that God didn't condemn him at all, but obviously there were consequences to his actions. I suggested he came by the soup kitchen any time he wanted and, if he felt like it, we could talk about it some more.

A few days later he turned up to see me. He was sweating, shaking and acting nervous. We chatted and he told me about his life. "I can't help you," I told him, "but Jesus can, if you surrender control of your life to Him." He said he would like some prayer, so I called Paul, a friend from church, and together we decided to go back with him to where he was staying.

Later, as we stood together in his room, I noticed that it seemed to be a very cold, emotionless place. There was a spiritual atmosphere; it felt unfriendly, unsympathetic; there was a heaviness in the room. I explained that Paul and I would pray for him and ask God to have His way. "Will Jesus heal me, Swanny?" he asked. "Just have faith in God," I told hm. "If you believe, then yes, He will heal you."

As we began to pray his body reacted physically. His head

involuntarily jerked from side to side, his shoulders twitched and his hands shook violently. It was unsettling to watch. I prayed that wherever there was darkness in his life, Jesus would bring His light. Paul prayed over and over that Jesus would pour His love into this young man. Suddenly, there was a noticeable change in the atmosphere. The darkness was dispelled and peace flooded the room.

I opened my eyes and saw a different man standing in front of me. Gone was the wreck of a person with misfortune etched on his face. There was a peace and serenity about his appearance. His body language had changed. He spoke about the love and peace that God had just poured into him. We laughed and cried together all at the same time, because he had changed so dramatically. The sense of God's presence was overwhelming.

* * *

One Saturday morning I got up early to spend time with God while Rachel lay asleep in bed. Outside it was cold and dark, raining a torrent. I'd arranged to pick up a friend later that day and take him to a men's breakfast meeting at another church. After sitting quietly for a while I got up to go to the bathroom and had a sick feeling in my stomach. The name "Chris" flashed across my mind. It was a fleeting thing. I ignored it and carried on preparing for the day ahead.

Minutes later, I had the same unpleasant feeling in my stomach. The name Chris came into my mind for a second time. I did have a friend called Chris who I'd known for several years. I also remembered I'd heard he was currently going through a tough time. I felt that God was trying to get my attention and turn my thoughts towards him. I began to be concerned. Something wasn't right.

I woke Rachel up and told her what was going on. She told me I ought to follow up on it. I decided to call Chris. If he answered and sounded fine, then I'd just invite him to come to the men's breakfast too, I thought. I tried, but his phone went straight to message. I was a little relieved. It was still very early and he might not thank me for calling him at the crack of dawn on a Saturday. As I hung up though, the same stomach churning sensation returned. I knew then that God was showing me this was something more serious. There was something wrong with Chris. I told Rachel I was going to go round to his house and asked her to start praying.

As I pulled up outside Chris' house I noticed that every curtain was closed. I got out of the car and went to knock on his door. There was no answer. I knocked several times and then waited, but there was only silence. I decided to call his brother. Chris's sister-in-law answered and explained that her husband was away on business. I explained my concerns, but she said she'd seen Chris the previous day and he seemed fine.

I returned to knocking on Chris' door, hammering so hard I thought I must be waking up the entire street. Still nothing but silence. I opened the letter box and shouted through it: "Chris, it's Swanny. If you don't answer the door I'm going to kick it down!" I shouted several times. Although I thought I must be making a real nuisance of myself, I knew I had to keep knocking, keep shouting. I was on the brink of forcing my way in when I saw a shadow emerge in the hall. Chris was coming down the stairs. He opened the door, albeit very slowly.

"Chris," I said, "are you okay mate? What's going on?" He just looked at me with a vacant expression. He seemed to be in a trance. I stepped inside. Chris dumped himself down onto the stairs and sat with his head in his hands. Eventually he managed to tell me that he'd taken an overdose of pain killers, washed down with a cocktail of vodka and beer. Though this was clearly bad news, I felt the knot in my stomach release. God had sent me there to help Chris, He surely wasn't going to let him die now. I phoned his sister-in-law back and asked her to call an ambulance while I focused on Chris.

He was acting strangely and telling me he just wanted to sleep. He made his way upstairs and I followed him. The empty beer and vodka bottles and empty tablet strips bore out his story. There was also a carving knife sitting by the side of his bed. Chris tried to lie down, but I wouldn't let him. I worked hard to keep him awake and keep him moving until the paramedics arrived. When they turned up, they ran some tests and said he needed to go straight to hospital. "If your friend survives, he'll have you to thank for saving his life," one of them confided.

Later that day I had to work at the tattoo studio. What I really wanted to do was go and see how Chris was. I believed he would be fine and I wanted to tell him that it wasn't me who had saved his life, but God. God knew all about his problems. Later on I got the okay to visit and Rachel and I headed over to the hospital.

When we arrived Chris was awake with lots of tubes connected to him. I did my best to explain to him what had happened earlier that day. Although shaken by his experience, Chris believed that it must have been God who prompted me to turn up at his house. He told me he had cried out for help, even as he was trying to end his life. I told him that God had heard and responded. He asked me how he could overcome the problems in his life and I told him he first needed to make Jesus his Lord and Saviour. Once he did that, then he could meditate on God's Word and receive a new, inner strength. His mind could be renewed and he would have a different perspective on life.

"Chris," I said, "that void needs filling with Christ mate." I tried to explain to him that he would always feel empty inside until He let God occupy that space. Only then would he begin to discover who he was really supposed to be.

After our chat about Jesus, Chris smiled. There was a new look on his face, a look I've since seen many times after I've spoken about Christ. Maybe it's what hope looks like. Once he'd left the hospital, Chris began coming to church and a few weeks later became a Christian. He is now being healed from his hurts and pains. He's grown so much since that day. Just a year later he accompanied Rachel and me on a mission trip to Uganda. He is in good health and growing in his faith. What a transformation.

* * *

Rachel's granddad, Bill, was 93 when he gave his life to Jesus. I described him as a "hard man". Not hard in the sense of fighting and drinking, but hard on himself, hard with his wife and kids, hard with anyone in fact. He was born in Yorkshire during times when life was tough for everyone and I guess this shaped his character. He only had one set of clothes as a little boy and his family frequently went for days without eating. Occasionally, he told me, he would eat leaves off the trees, just to take away his hunger pains. They were truly poor. Life was hard.

When he was just 10, his dad took him to one side and told him it was time for him to become a man and survive in the world on his own wits, adding that, "real men don't cry." So he learned to grow up fast. At 14 he began his working life coal mining down in the pits of Yorkshire. By the time Bill was a young man he was going off to fight in the war, along with thousands of others.

Bill had lived a whole lifetime before I knew him. At the age of 93 he began to have some health problems. His doctor sent him into hospital for some tests and Rachel and I would go and visit him. I would sit by his bed and tell him all about my faith. Bill would listen and sometimes ask questions. He told me he'd been given a Bible as a young man – everyone did who joined the army. He'd been to church at times over the years, but admitted he didn't have any kind of relationship with God.

I would say to him, "Anyone who calls on God for help can be saved, Bill." He'd just nod and reply flatly, "Oh right, I didn't know that." Occasionally I'd ask if he wanted me to pray with him, but he'd always say, "I don't think Jesus would be interested in me, Swanny. I've not been the best of men." I'd told him that God loved him regardless; all he needed to do was ask God to forgive his sins.

One day Bill was taken in for x-rays and the results revealed two cancerous growths at the top of his bowel. He needed an operation quickly as one was particularly large. He was scheduled for surgery just a day later. Everyone was concerned because of his age.

The next morning Rachel and I went out training together as we sometimes do. While we were running I felt God speak to me. He said we needed to go to the hospital right away and pray and lay hands on Bill. We dropped what we were doing and went.

When we arrived there Bill was sleeping. When he woke up he asked how long we'd been there. I told him we'd just arrived because God had told us to come and see him. "Well, what does He want?" he asked in his blunt Yorkshire way; a man of few words. "I don't know, Bill," I told him, "but He said to come and put my hands on you and pray. Maybe He's going to heal you." Unfazed by this he simply said, "Get on with it then." Rachel and I prayed for him and asked God to keep His hand on Bill throughout the operation. Then we kissed him and left the hospital. We drove away feeling confident that God was up to something.

That night Rachel had a phone call from her mum. She said that the surgeons had opened Bill up to remove the growths, but there was no cancer to be found in his body. They were completely puzzled, but the evidence was clear, so they stitched him back up and sent him back to the ward. Rachel's mum had questioned the surgeons about this and the x-rays that had clearly shown the growths. They said they didn't understand it; there must have been "some mistake". She could hardly believe what she was hearing. We knew that God had touched Bill. Then Rachel's mum said that Bill wanted to see me; he had something to tell me.

The next day visiting time came around and Rachel and I were back at the hospital. What Bill told me took my faith to a new level. He explained that while he was under anaesthetic, he'd met Jesus and that he'd held His hand. Bill's eyes were shining brightly. They had a new look about them. He glowed as he told us what happened. We were all full of joy, thanking God for what He'd done.

After this, Bill was a completely different man, full of God's presence. He would frequently talk to me about Jesus and told other patients on the ward to get to know Him before it was too late!

Rachel laughed. "Only Jesus could do this to my granddad," she said. "Only Jesus could do this to anyone," I replied. After that day I'd often go with my Bible and read Bill stories about Jesus. He'd lie and listen, we'd talk for hours, and on many occasions the nurses let us stay until nearly midnight; way past visiting hours. He'd tell us all about his life, especially his time during the war, and it was a pleasure to listen and to get to know him more. Sadly, a couple of months later he passed away. He is sorely missed, but we have great joy knowing that he's now in heaven.

Why God healed Bill from cancer and then took him home shortly after I don't know; only God knows the answer. I'm just grateful that he left this life in peace, knowing Jesus. Wherever you are in your life right now, I encourage you to invite God to take charge of your life and carry your burdens. The Bible says that, "Everyone who calls on the name of the Lord will be saved" (Romans 10:13). Are you ready to walk in His direction?

17

NEW ADVENTURES

When a person entrusts their life to God, He is able to erase the old story of their life – filled as it may be with many pages of pain, despair, fear or whatever – and He writes a new story. God always had a script for my life that was radically different to the one I was living. This story told a different tale; it went in a completely different direction. It was a good story. Looking back, if anyone had told the old Swanny about some of the things he would see and do in the future, he would have laughed in their face. It would have seemed too far fetched. Write a book, me? You're joking. Run a soup kitchen? Forget it! Go on missions to Africa? You're off your head mate! And yet, here I am...

I didn't know it, but God had adventures waiting with my name on them. I've since been privileged to travel to many places around the world. Africa is one of the special places; completely unexpected, yet in the end, so right. I'd like to share some of the stories with you.

Kenya

Kenya is a nation that has become close to my heart. Rachel and I went on holiday there before either of us became a Christian. We saw many breathtakingly beautiful things there, but were struck by the poverty that abounds. To see it on the TV is one thing; to experience it first hand is something altogether different. It was heart breaking to see. I found it so confusing that the world is so out of balance; why some places have so much and others so little. There didn't seem to be a satisfactory explanation. On that trip I think I spent more time outside our hotel chatting to the locals than I spent inside. The people touched my heart. As we flew back home I found myself saying to Rachel, "This won't be the last time we visit here. Next time we'll be coming back to help." It was a strange thing to say, I guess. Little did I know that God had planned just that.

Four years after we became Christians, Rachel and I decided to return to Kenya for a holiday and take the kids with us. We had a great time there and on one of the days chose to go on safari into the Masai Mara. Afterwards we were waiting for our plane to take us back to Mombasa to spend the rest of our holiday at a beach hotel. While we were waiting we got chatting to a lady from Nairobi. God showed me that she had come out to the Masai Mara to run away from problems she was having at home. I stepped out in faith and told her that I was a Christian, saying that God had shown me her pain. She was very surprised, but told me that what I was saying was true – she was there to escape. I did my best to explain that running away would never solve her problems because she was carrying them inside. I told her some of my story and explained how for years I'd tried to run, unsuccessfully, from my pain. Until Christ came to help me I just kept on running. She cried and told me that she didn't know what else to do. I told her a story from the Bible.

Abram and Sarai were promised a child by God, even though Sarai was beyond childbearing age. Instead of trusting God to work this problem out, Abram went and slept with his servant, Hagar. It was a man-made solution to a problem God had already promised to deal with. It caused all sorts of problems. This is what happens when we try to deal with difficult situations on our own, excluding God from the equation. Instead we need to ask for His help and then trust Him.

In the biblical account, in spite of the mess Abram and Sarai got into, God was still faithful to them and demonstrated His ability to work out every situation for good. I told this lady that, in the same way, if she would put her trust in God, He would be able to help her. She understood and asked if we would pray with her. She asked Jesus to come into her life and to help solve her problems. Rachel gave her a Bible to take away with her. "No problem is too complicated for God," I said, "if you're willing to let Him help you."

God has the same message for us today. If we run from our problems, they follow us anyway. Instead, we need to ask God to help us through them and trust in His love and commitment to us.

Prior to going to Kenya, Rachel and I had visited a company in Ireland who print Bibles and individual gospels in many different languages. The people who run it told me that if I ever wanted books to give away to others, they would send me copies of the New Testament Gospel of John. They were true to their word and so we went to Kenya armed with loads of them to give away. The day after returning from the safari I had chance to begin handing them out.

We were sitting around the pool having fun and enjoying the sun when all of a sudden I felt God ask me to go and speak to some of the lads who worked down on the beach. He wanted me to tell them about His love. I told Rachel that I was going to talk to them, but wanted her and the kids to stay in the grounds of the hotel where it was safe. Tourists weren't advised to go wandering down there alone.

I'd learnt that a lot of the lads in the area were practicing witchcraft. As a result there was a lot of spiritual darkness surrounding the area around the beach. I had to scramble over and jump down from a high wall that separated the beach from the hotel grounds. Almost immediately, from nowhere a group of lads appeared and rushed up to me. Some were trying to sell things; others wanted to take me on trips to different places. They got quite aggressive with one another as they vied for my attention, pushing, shoving and shouting. It had the potential to be quite intimidating, but it didn't faze me. Meanwhile, Rachel was watching everything, peering over the edge of the wall.

Eventually I shouted for them to be quiet and told them I wanted to speak. I told them I wasn't there to give them money; I wanted to give them the good news about Jesus. They all stopped talking and began to listen. I told them that darkness could be a stronghold in their lives and control them, taking them into situations where they didn't really want to go. But Jesus said, "I am the light of the world. Whoever follows me will never walk in darkness, but will have the light of life" (John 8:12). The darkness, I said, will never overcome God's light. We are all lost, in need of a Saviour, but when we come to Jesus, He can light our path and show us how to live our life. When Christ is your light, you need never stumble in darkness.

The lads took in all I was saying. I was on a roll, like a seasoned preacher! I told them that though they may feel poor, naturally speaking, if they asked Jesus into their lives the Holy Spirit would come into their hearts and bring an inner richness that could not be compared to earthly wealth. As I said these words, one by one, unbidden, they dropped to their knees, closed their eyes and lifted their hands towards heaven. I said a prayer which they could repeat and every one of them asked Jesus to come into his life. I called up to Rachel and she began handing down copies of John's Gospel to me and I gave one to each of them. They laughed and hugged me and each other.

One of the lads, called Abraham, told me he'd given his heart to Jesus a few years before, but temptations had dragged him back into his old life. However, a week before Rachel and I arrived in Kenya he had a dream one night. In the dream he saw a man come to the beach wearing a white top (I was wearing a white vest) and speak to him, reminding him that his life belonged to God. The man had copies of the Bible in his hand, which were being handed down to him from above by someone else. He couldn't believe that what he'd seen in his dream was happening now, right in front of him. He knew God must have sent us.

Afterwards, Rachel and I went back to relaxing in the sunshine. Every day after that the lads came back wanting me to tell them more about God. They asked many questions and listened intently. They brought friends who wanted to know God and we gave them Bibles too. On Sunday that week, Abraham invited us to go to a local mud hut church. When we arrived the pastor had arranged for all the children from the local community to welcome us with songs. It was very humbling. Then he invited me to get up and preach! I was amazed that God had planned all of this beforehand. I'm still in touch with Abraham to this day and he often writes to tell me that God is using him to touch the lives of others.

Uganda

A week or so after I became a Christian I was talking to Pastor Paul and he told me that Beacon Christian Centre had a connection with Uganda. He said that if I ever wanted to get involved with this project I was more than welcome. It sounded exciting, so I told him to count me in.

In 2000 Paul was out in Uganda on a mission trip when he met a local pastor called Joseph. Joseph took him to a place where he'd nailed together some old wooden pallets to make two school "classrooms". God had given him a vision, he explained, to one day build a school there connected to a large church that would serve the community. There would be many brick classrooms, an administration block, a dining hall and sleeping dormitories for the children. Whilst Joseph was explaining this, God filled Paul's heart with the same vision. Back in England, Paul shared this with the church and everyone decided they should do whatever they could to help build it.

On my first trip to see the project I was amazed by how much work had been done and by the sacrificial giving of the people of Beacon church and surrounding area that had helped make it happen. I felt privileged to play some small part in seeing the school become a reality. It is called "Alpha and Omega". The children who attend range from three to fourteen years of age and are lovely. Some have no parents to care for them. Others have only one parent and are extremely poor. Others have HIV/AIDS. The dormitories are used by the neediest of the 200-plus children who attend the school. The orphans have to rely on their extended families and sponsors from the UK to take care of them. Despite their dire circumstances, the children always have smiles on their faces. They are always laughing and playing, singing songs about God, praising Jesus for His love. This always humbles anyone who visits them.

In contrast to these kids who, though very poor, are being looked after, there are the village children who don't attend the school. Their stomachs are distended due to malnutrition. Their families have nothing. The few clothes that they wear are more like rags, hanging from their frail bodies. No one has any shoes. If I ever catch myself complaining about something trivial, I quickly remind myself of these children. As the saying goes, "I thought I was hard-done-to having no shoes, until I came across the man who had no feet."

Seeing the poverty in a nation like Uganda has an effect on you. I've had some life-changing conversations there too, which God has used to change my perspective on life. Once I was chatting to a local Christian man. I was feeling sorry for the people who live there, because they have so little, and I told him so. His response amazed me. "The people in the West often feel sympathy for us, because we have nothing," he told me. "But when we have God we have everything." Then came the crunch: "We feel sorry for you. We see so much unhappiness inside the people who live in the West. The richness of life can't be found in material things; the richness of life lies within us. That is where the Kingdom of Heaven is. There is nothing wrong with having nice things, Swanny. But don't make them your God."

It is said that the eyes are the window to the soul. I found it easy to look into the eyes of Ugandan brothers and sisters, because they were transparent – not clouded by cares, not weighed down by possessions. They had nothing to hide. So many people I meet don't have that transparency. They have a look, a stare, that reveals the true condition of their soul; healthy on the outside they are starved of life within. Spiritual poverty is as heart breaking as physical poverty. If only we would all stop wearing our masks and be real! But we have too many things to hide behind in the West. This is why I have such a burning desire to tell people how they can be free.

On another occasion, Pastor Paul and I were doing some building work on the school. Part way through the morning we decided to have a break. We had some bread and crisps, so decided to make the obligatory crisp sandwich. I had my sandwich literally hovering near my mouth when out of the corner of my eye I noticed a little girl, dressed in rags, staring at me. Her clothes were torn and her belly swollen with malnutrition. I couldn't bring myself to eat the sandwich, so I held it out to her. She was hesitant at first, but I encouraged her to take it and she eventually did. I expected her to eat it there and then, but she didn't and quickly ran off. Curious, I followed a little way behind to see what she would do.

I saw her as she ran over to three other starving children. I don't know who they were, friends, family perhaps. Without hesitation she broke the sandwich into four equal parts and shared it out. The sight of this arrested me and my eyes stung with tears. I cried at her selfless generosity.

The Ugandan people have taught me a lot about faith. They encourage me to thank God more often for what I have got and not complain about what I haven't got. We can have everything in the world's eyes and yet still be lost. If my friends, Tyler and Louise, hadn't been faithful to God in telling me about Him, I may never have heard about Jesus; never had the opportunity to do something positive to help the lives of others; never seen a little girl share a crisp sandwich in desperate circumstances, despite her own hunger.

* * *

Each year a team from the church will go out to Uganda and do various things to help the project to thrive. Some help in the school teaching Maths and English. We educate the kids regarding their health, hygiene and sexual health in the light of the HIV/AIDS epidemic. Some teach sports or IT. I will usually be involved sharing the gospel at crusades.

On one occasion, Pastor Paul asked if I'd like to help him baptise 42 people in Lake Victoria. I jumped at the offer. It was an overwhelmingly breath-taking experience, waist deep in water, seeing person after person plunge below the water and come up smiling, a new person. It wasn't until we'd finished that someone told me they admired me for my bravery. It was well known locally that the lake was completely crocodile infested! Nevertheless, it was an incredibly special moment.

One last story... the youngest daughter of Pastor Joseph and his wife, Ruth, is called Keturah. Aged around 10, she had a fear of water and couldn't swim, even though she really longed to. One day I told her that the opposite of fear is faith. "Faith and fear can't exist together," I told her, "so if you have faith, then fear has to go." I reminded her of the story of Jesus walking out across the water to His disciples, who were huddled in their boat in a storm. He told them not to be afraid. One of the disciples,

Peter, said, "Lord, if it is you then tell me to come to you on the water" (Matthew 14:28). Jesus encouraged him to step out in faith, so he did. He walked on the water towards Jesus. For a moment, however, he took his eyes off Jesus and looked at the high waves and the wind. As soon as he did this he was terrified and began to sink. Jesus had to grab him and save him. Peter should have kept his focus on Jesus. I explained all of this to Keturah and said that if she had faith instead of fear, God would give her a new-found confidence in Him and she'd be able to swim. She told me she understood exactly what I was saying.

On one of our rest days we decided to go swimming. Keturah was there and I encouraged her to get in the water with me and keep her mind focused on Jesus. "Have faith," I said. She looked at me warily, but began to walk slowly into the water. Once in, I held her up and allowed her to move her arms and legs while I supported her. "Faith or fear, Keturah?" I asked as she splashed around. "I have faith, Swanny!" she called back. Minutes later I let go of her and she continued to swim unaided. "Look Mama!" she called to Ruth. "I'm swimming!"

"I know you are, Keturah," her mother called back. "Swanny isn't even holding you any more."

"I know he isn't Mama," she yelled, "Jesus is. He's holding me up because I have faith."

This simple story illustrates how God feels about each one of us and what He wants us to do. He wants us to be free from fear; free to be and do all we're supposed to. He is passionate about our freedom. And He wants us to trust in Him; to trust enough to step out and believe that He will hold us up. He will, because He never fails and will never let us fall.

18

ENCOURAGEMENT FOR THE JOURNEY

It's early morning and I've just finished spending some quiet time with God. I have sat in His presence, read the Bible, and listened to what He wanted to say to me. I have told him how much I appreciate having Him in my life and I've thanked Him for helping me to write this book. It has been challenging, to try to articulate my story and put it into words. It has brought back many memories. I pray that you have been encouraged and helped by what you've read.

Life has been quite a journey so far. In my past, I did a lot of bad things I regretted and have had to pay the consequences for my actions. I've experienced a lot of heartache, but I thank God for helping me to change my way of thinking and discover my true identity in Christ. I know I'm still far from perfect, but I also know that God is for me and through His strength I'll be guided into a brighter future.

Christ lived on the earth and died on the cross for our sins, so that whoever believes and trusts in Him can have a better life than this one, eternally in heaven. The Bible says if you look for Him, you will find Him. All you need to do is ask.

The Old Testament tells the story of how God's people were so close to entering the land He had promised to them, but talked themselves out of entering it because of fear. They put their destiny on hold for 40 years and wandered around in the wilderness, just because they were afraid, with no real evidence to support their fears. God has a great plan for your life; don't deny yourself the joy and adventure of following God because you're afraid of what might happen.

So often people allow themselves to be deceived by negative self-talk. Don't ever think that God couldn't be interested in someone like you. If He was interested in redeeming me, then he's interested in doing it for you! Don't believe anyone who says you'll never amount to anything or achieve your dreams. God's opinion of you is completely different. He will help you to overcome any obstacles that stand in the way of you living the life He has planned for you.

If you are a believer, then I encourage you to invest time spent in God's presence. Fill your mind with God's Word. When your mind is full of truth, there is no room for worries and fear. Instead we become full of peace and freedom. In the book of Joshua we read that God says, "Do not be terrified; do not be discouraged for the Lord your God will be with you wherever you go" (Joshua 1:9) and elsewhere we read: "If God is for us, who can be against us?" (Romans 8:31). In Isaiah we read, "Those who hope in the Lord will renew their strength, they will soar on wings like eagles, they will run and not grow weary, they will walk and not be faint" (Isaiah 40:31). The greatest lesson I've learned in my life is that God's strength is our only true source of strength. Man was created to depend on Him because He created us. When we break that equation and rely on our own strength or cleverness or resourcefulness – no matter how good we think we are – we are doomed to failure. With God's strength, however, we can achieve incredible things. We can make it through even the most intense storms that life throws at us and we won't crack or crumble under the pressure.

If life has been, or is still, tough for you, be encouraged. Our weakness is our greatest strength. When we come to the end of ourselves and all our natural resources are exhausted, this is when God can step in and accomplish a miracle. Whatever has happened on your journey of life, God can bring you through it and make you a whole person.

I always carry this little note in my wallet. It reads as follows:

"Don't settle for just achieving the good life, because the good life isn't good enough. It doesn't satisfy. You can have a lot to live on and still have nothing to live for. Aim instead for the better life; serving God in a way that expresses your heart. Figure out what you love to do, what God gave you the heart to do, and then do it for His glory."

As the pastor Bill Johnson once said regarding the Christian life, "It's not a made-up lifestyle; it's a lifestyle for which we are made." I will never stop giving glory and thanks to God for what He has done for me. It seems so long ago now that the small 10-year old "lost boy" was beaten and sexually abused on a daily basis. The feelings associated with those times are now a distant memory. It has been an extremely tough journey – one that has taken me to depths I could never have imagined. But now, through Christ, God has taken me to heights I could never have imagined either. He has taken what was evil and turned it into something good, as only He can. I have tried to tell you, with weak, faltering words, what it is like to experience God's love, but really you must experience it for yourself. Take a leap of faith and you will find yourself living the most adventurous, peaceful, joyful life imaginable.

There is a passage in the book of Isaiah, chapter 49, that speaks prophetically about the birth of Jesus and what He will accomplish on earth when He is born. Like most passages in the Bible, it has a meaning relating to the context in which it was written, but then God uses those words to speak directly into our lives now. This whole passage talks amazingly about how God knows us by name, even before we are born, and has a distinct purpose for our lives. He knew everything about every one of us, whilst we were still in our mother's womb. This is God's way of telling us that He had good plans prepared for our lives all along. Before a single word of our life story was written, He knew and loved us.

The course the first half of my life ran was no surprise to God. Then, the course it has taken since He stepped into it is no surprise to Him either. He knew all along. I want to leave you with the thought that God has known you right from the beginning. He has had a joy-filled, peace-filled life mapped out for you all along. All you need to do is let Him take control of your life and help you live it. For years I was locked up in a prison of my own making – a prison without bars. But as soon as I stopped trying to break out in my own strength and surrendered my life to Him, God was able to release me; release to a future of unlimited possibilities in His love and power.

"If the Son sets you free, you will be free indeed." (John 8:36)

EPILOGUE:
THE NEXT STEP
IS YOURS

If you are not a Christian reading this book and it has touched you, and you'd like to ask Jesus into your life, I invite you to pray the following prayer:

"Lord God, I come to you in the name of Jesus Christ.

Your Word says that anyone who calls on the name of the Lord will be saved.

Please come into my heart and forgive me of all my sins.

Thank you for loving me and giving me a new life in Christ.

Amen."

If you have prayed this prayer sincerely, I want to say congratulations – you are now a child of God! I strongly recommend that you find a Christian church in your community. Go and speak to the leaders, tell them you've said this salvation prayer, and say you'd like to attend the church as a new Christian and learn to grow in your faith.

God Bless you,

Swanny.

Swanny and Rachel

Swanny and the Soup Kitchen gang (see p143)

Swanny and Chris (see p151)

Baptisms in a crocodile infested river in Uganda (see p167)

Salvation on the beach in Kenya (see p162)